MW00852584

IN SEARCH OF THE
NEW FOREST
COVEN

By The Same Author:

Skyways and Landmarks Revisited
(with Jimmy Goddard and Paul Baines) (1985)

Earth Mysteries: An Exploratory Introduction
(with Brian Larkman) (1985)

Tony Wedd: New Age Pioneer (1986)

The Elements of Earth Mysteries (1991)

Secret Places of the Goddess (1995)

Earth Mysteries (1995)

Mirrors of Magic (1997)

Magical Guardians (1998)

Leylines: A Beginner's Guide (1999)

Wiccan Roots (2000)

Gerald Gardner and the Cauldron of Inspiration (2003)

Newland Avenue School 1896-2006 (2006)

Witchfather: A Life of Gerald Gardner (Vols. 1 and 2) (2012)

Doreen Valiente Witch (2016)

IN SEARCH OF THE
NEW FOREST COVEN

by

Philip Heselton

Published by Fenix Flames Publishing Ltd 2020

Copyright © 2020   Philip Heselton

All rights reserved including the right of reproduction in whole or in part in any form. No reproduction, copy or transmission of this publication may be made without written permission. No paragraph of this publication may be reproduced, copied or transmitted save with written permission or in accordance with the provisions of the Copyright Act 1956 (as amended). Any person who performs any unauthorised act in relation to this publication may be liable to criminal prosecution and civil claims for damages. The moral rights of the author have been asserted.

Published by Fenix Flames Publishing Ltd

Design, Layout & illustrations: Ashley Mortimer

Printed by Lightning Source International / Ingram Spark

Paperback ISBN 978-1-913768-00-3
Hardback ISBN 978-1-913768-02-7
Digital book   ISBN 978-1-913768-01-0

www.publishing.fenixflames.co.uk

For

Sarah Louise Kay

9th April 1992 - 5th January 2019

Contents

Illustrations

Picture Credits

British Federation of the International Order of Co-Freemasonry, Le Droit Humaine, 14; Crown Copyright, 49; Laura-Beth Dawson, cover photography; Google Street View, 30; George Knowles, 37; Ian Stevenson Archive Trust, 39, 42, 43; Pam Mason, 40; Muriel Pécastaing-Boissière, 21; TammyLyn Shaw, dedication page; Keith Thompson, 2, 5, 6, 7, 8, 9, 22; Bill Wakefield, 17, 18; The author, 1, 8, 10, 13, 28, 29, 32, 33, 36, 46, 47, 48. All other illustrations are in the collection of the author.

The author and publishers have made every effort to identify copyright holders and to obtain their permission but would be glad to hear of any inadvertent errors or omissions.

Author's Acknowledgements

A book such as this tends to be the result of many items of information from a great variety of sources. Many people have helped me with this, some helping a lot and others just providing a snippet of information which helps to build up the whole picture. I am therefore not distinguishing individual contributions but am grateful to all who gave freely of their knowledge, expertise or time. They include:

Jo Anderson; Mary Allen; Paul Atkin; Julie Belham Payne; Geraldine Beskin; Sophia Boann; Gavin Bone; Lesley-Anne Brewster; Hilary Byers; John Callow; Francis Cameron; Mike Cherry; Ann Cook; Patricia Crowther; Laura-Beth Dawson; Janet Farrar; Robert A Gilbert; Richard Gordon; Amanda Greenwood; Clive Harper; Christina Oakley Harrington; Melissa and Rufus Harrington; Nigel and Susan Heselton; Moira Hodgkinson; Dave Holley; Ronald Hutton; IAPSOP; Dave James; Richard James; Tamarra James; Paul Johnson; Evelyn Juers; Aidan Kelly; George Knowles; Grevel Lindop; Chris Lycett; Mary Kay Mahoney; Gareth Medway; Ashley Mortimer; Muriel Pécastaing-Boissière; Leslie Price; Daru Rooke; Melissa Seims; TammyLyn Shaw; Rebecca Somerset; Ian Stevenson; Tim Stimson; Jonathan Tapsell; David Thomas; Alan Thorogood; William Wallworth; Rowan Wulfe; Jenny Wylam.

I would also like to acknowledge the contributions of the following individuals who have now passed through the veil:

Gurth Brooke; Amanda Class-Hamilton; Maidie Doohan; Raven Grimassi; Ralph Harvey; Joan and Kenneth Heselton; Michael Howard; Louise Jennings; Sarah Louise Kay; Fred Lamond; Bill Wakefield.

I am sure that, with the number of contributions to this book, that I will have missed someone from this list. This is the result of my failing memory rather than the value of their contributions.

Foreword

We are right on the edge of a mysterious forest, full of enigmas and contradictions. I am fortunate to have spoken with the very last of those who knew the individuals involved in this story. Indeed, several of those have now passed through the veil, and I feel a willing duty fall upon me to record what they told me, thus shining at least some light on that early period of what we now refer to as Wicca but which the earliest members knew as 'the witch cult'.

In about 1959, I borrowed a book entitled *Witchcraft Today* from my well-stocked local library.[1] It was by one Gerald B. Gardner. On the title page, under the author's name, appeared the following:

> *Member of one of the ancient covens of the Witch Cult which still survive in England.*

 That one phrase resonated with me deeply. It suggested forgotten or strangely remote parts of the countryside, where members of old farming families met in isolated barns or in the corners of fields to practise age-old rituals with antlers and fires in cauldrons to mark the passage of the year or to perform magical rites to influence some event in their everyday lives.

My investigations, which started some 20 years ago now, were directed towards examining that statement. The truth turned out to be only partly that; but this was the vision that caused me to want to find out more about those "surviving witch covens", and that desire set me off on a journey which I am still on.

I was inspired to continue my researches by the work of Doreen Valiente, Professor Ronald Hutton and the late Mike Howard,

---

[1]   Gerald B. Gardner *Witchcraft Today* (Rider, 1954).

editor of that well-respected journal, *The Cauldron*. I wrote Wiccan Roots as a first attempt at a history.[2]

Several books later, I feel that, though there is still much mystery, I am getting closer to what may have happened. I have found, and placed in position, several pieces of this large and intricate jigsaw puzzle. I know that it is by no means complete, but the current volume aims to fill in the picture to a significant extent and there is much here that has not previously been published.

My approach in research for, and writing, the present volume has been to find out as much as I can about the individuals who have been mentioned as having been involved in the group into which Gerald Gardner was initiated. This would include not only their esoteric interests (and most had quite a few!) but also their more everyday lives, personalities and characters; to bring them alive, so to speak.

My aim in writing this book is to get a clearer idea of how they met each other and the extent to which they developed a joint practice and belief which came together to form something into which Gardner could be initiated.

I started by having a look at the written sources which Gardner has left us. These include his books, both fiction and non-fiction, published and unpublished; his letters; 'Books of Shadows'; interviews and newspaper reports; and accounts by those who knew him. These give various clues and information which enable us to piece together an idea of what the group into which he was initiated was like.

The most comprehensive account of the events leading up to Gardner's initiation is given in a biography published in 1960. Less than four years before Gardner's death in 1964 at the age of 79, *Gerald Gardner Witch* was published.[3] The evidence seems to indicate that much of the book is actually in Gardner's own words,

---

2   Philip Heselton *Wiccan Roots* (Capall Bann, 2000).

3   J. L. Bracelin *Gerald Gardner Witch* (Octagon 1960).

probably based on recorded interviews and therefore it is close to being an autobiography. That book has been most valuable in providing details of Gardner's life between his birth in 1884 and his initiation in 1939. Admittedly the author gets certain details wrong, but it is a valuable resource nonetheless, and it reads as being a truthful account of remarkable events.

The part of the account in *Gerald Gardner Witch* that I was most interested in for the present purposes is, appropriately enough, Chapter 13, which is entitled "Into the Witch Cult". As it provides the fullest and most relevant start to our enquiry, I quote extensively from that chapter. It gives several clues which we will follow up on in subsequent chapters of this book. Taking the relevant sections of Chapter 13 of Gerald Gardner Witch we can look at the essence of the story, as told in Gardner's own words, from the time of his retirement to England in 1936 to his initiation in 1939.

As the result of my researches I have found that certain of the author's statements are inaccurate, possibly through misinterpretation of what Gardner had told him. Having become familiar with Gardner's personality, I suspect that some of that misinterpretation may have been deliberate intention on Gardner's part.

I have been accused by some of accepting without question Gardner's story of how he met the witches and underwent initiation.[4] But, whilst I never met him, I have, in the course of my researches, got to know him surprisingly well.

In the whole of his writings it is rare to find a deliberate untruth. He may have believed things which were subsequently found to be untrue, and faithfully reproduced them. Gerald was, however, a master at giving misleading impressions whilst telling the literal

---

[4]   Chas S Clifton 'Mouse's Way: Philip Heselton's Biographies of Gerald Gardner', *Letter from Hardscrabble Creek. A Pagan Writer's Blog* (12 January 2013)[http://blog.chasclifton.com/?p=5032]

truth. He was a trickster of the first magnitude and I give some examples of his skill in that direction.

Someone who knew Gerald well, and who was a member of his Bricket Wood coven, was Fred Lamond. Writing about Gerald, he told me:

> *People with creative imaginations don't always lie, however: the problem is discovering which of their stories are true and which are not.*[5]

I have to say that, in studying Gerald Gardner Witch, I have found that, where it can be checked, the story as told by Gardner is in all major respects effectively true.

I think I know Gerald Gardner sufficiently well to be sure that his account of what was the most important event in his life is basically true. Of course, even here he is adept at giving misleading impressions, as we shall see in due course. And, in certain respects, he was, as we probably all are, good at fooling himself: to be guilty of wishful thinking. Undoubtedly I will also have got some things wrong, particularly where I have engaged in speculation.

To start with, I decided to look more closely at the group of people into which retired civil servant, Gerald Gardner, said he had been initiated, because I had the strong suspicion that those who stated that Gardner had made the whole thing up were wrong. Undoubtedly he had made some of it up, as did many of those who will appear in the pages of this book. Indeed, this is its main theme: that the Craft has evolved over time since the early years of the 20th Century through the contributions of individuals.

They were mostly middle class middle-aged women who were interested in the occult: that which lies hidden behind everyday reality. And they were mostly living in the vicinity of Highcliffe-on-Sea, a village on the edge of the New Forest.

---

[5] Email Frederic Lamond to the author Friday 24 October 2003.

It would be good to be able to go back and hear the conversations they had and see what they were actually doing. But, in the absence of that ability, I have tried to bring the various characters to life as best I can. It has involved gathering small snippets of information from a wide variety of sources, and new sources have been made available in recent years which have proved very useful indeed. It is indeed exciting when two pieces of the jigsaw puzzle from totally different sources fit together.

Early on in my investigations I began to realise that this was not a coven surviving from mediaeval times but one which seemed more to be a product of the 20th Century. It is a case of those with particular interests and experiences coming across each other, sharing those interests and, through what has been called a fertilising cauldron of inspiration, seeing those interests combine and begin to focus on a thread of witchcraft.

They all seemed to be firm believers in reincarnation, which became a central feature in the rich mix of themes which became 'the witch cult'. It appeared to start, some time in the mid-1930s, when at least two of the company who had memories of being a witch in a previous lifetime said "We believe we have been witches in a previous lifetime; we can therefore be witches in our present lifetime".

Timothy Landry[6] told me: *I was talking to a Craft friend the other day and he described Wicca as a reincarnation cult rather than a fertility cult. It resonated with me.*

It resonated with me as well, and I think Gardner felt the same, since he wrote an article, as yet unpublished, entitled 'Reincarnation as the witch religion'.[7] I don't believe now that a group of people sat around one evening and decided to form a 'witch cult'. It started, I think, when more than one individual revealed to their group of friends that they thought that one of their ancestors had

---

[6] Facebook, 2 October 2018.

[7] Gerald Gardner - article in the Toronto collection.

been a witch or that they themselves had memories of being a witch in a previous lifetime. I will elaborate on this later.

I feel I have to emphasise that it was not their religion, at least not to start with. Most of them remained Christian all their lives, or at any rate put things in such wider context as the Theosophical Society promulgated. Witchcraft was merely one thread in the rich tapestry of occult and esoteric endeavour, though for Gardner, and I think for some of the others, it later became more.

In many ways, I am saying nothing new. Over 20 years ago, Professor Ronald Hutton, in his book *The Triumph of the Moon* had set out most of the influences that led ultimately to what he called modern pagan witchcraft.[8] What I have done is to investigate the evolutionary nature of this process and to put names and some faces to the individuals involved. There is much to do before the picture, even in its broad outline, is complete. This volume focuses on some of the people involved. I hope at some stage to write further about the beliefs and practices of those members of the witch cult who, in 1939, called themselves 'the wica'.

---

[8] Ronald Hutton *The Triumph of the Moon* (Oxford University Press, 1999; Revised edition 2019).

1

The Witch Cult

It certainly started with Gerald Gardner. Which is not to say that he invented it, but he it was who brought it into the open and made people aware of its existence. So much so that it acquired the name of 'Gardnerian' witchcraft, first as a derogatory epithet and then later as pure description of a path that now has many hundreds of thousands of followers, in Britain and around the world.

So, who was Gerald Gardner? I suppose I am bound to draw attention to my own two-volume biography of Gardner entitled *Witchfather*,[1] but for the present purposes, a short summary will suffice.

Gerald Brosseau Gardner (1884-1964) was born into a well-to-do hardwood timber importing family based in Liverpool. As a child he had asthma. In those days the only way to alleviate that condition was to move to warmer climes. So, as the Gardners could afford it, they sent Gerald with his nursemaid/governess, 'Com' (Georgiana McCombie) to Madeira for several years running, returning to England only for the summer months.

It seems as if Gerald did not receive much tuition from Com, but he had an enquiring mind and managed to teach himself to read. He also acquired a life-long interest in and collection of knives.

Gerald spent his working life 'out East', first as a tea planter in Ceylon (Sri Lanka) and then as a rubber planter in Borneo (Sabah) and Johore (Malaysia). He ended up as a government inspector of chandu (opium) shops.

---

[1] Philip Heselton *Witchfather: A Life of Gerald Gardner* 2 vols. (Thoth Publications, 2012).

Developing his interest in knives to study the Malayan kris, he wrote his first book, entitled *Keris and Other Malay Weapons*[2] in 1936. He also became a keen amateur archaeologist, finding evidence by excavation of sea-going Malay vessels.

Gerald retired in 1936 at the age of 52 and returned to England, finding a flat at 23a Buckingham Palace Mansions, a large block of flats dating from the 1880s, now demolished, right across the road from Victoria Station in London. Bracelin takes up the story:

> *Civil defence plans were that in the event of war, every house within half a mile of each large London railway station was to be evacuated. The flat which he shared with his wife was just across the road from Victoria terminus: and he was determined that his collection should not be destroyed. The only place in England where he had friends was the region of the New Forest, and he managed to get a house there, where wife and collection were duly installed.*[3]

The friends that Bracelin refers to were probably, but not certainly, Gerald's old nursemaid, Com, and her husband, David, who were living in retirement in Bournemouth.

Gerald soon found, and bought, a large detached house, Southridge, in Highcliffe, a seaside village near Christchurch in Hampshire, not far from the New Forest or from Bournemouth.

He had been a naturist (nudist) since finding the benefit of sunlight on his skin in aiding the healing process when he was out East. Having settled in Highcliffe, he soon joined the New Forest Club situated at Rushford Warren, Mudeford, on the banks of Christchurch Harbour.

---

[2] G B Gardner *Keris and Other Malay Weapons* (Progressive Publishing Company, Singapore, 1936).

[3] Bracelin p. 159.

1. Southridge - Gerald Gardner's house in Highcliffe 1938-1945

Bracelin comments:

It was the end of the year; the naturist club which he had joined was closed for the winter, and he was thrown upon his own resources. On one of his long cycle rambles, Gardner came across a curious building in Christchurch. Cut in the stone the legend said: THE FIRST ROSICRUCIAN THEATRE IN ENGLAND. Later he was to find out what this meant. This was the discovery which led to his recruitment into the cult of the witches.[4]

The theatre which Gerald discovered was run by the Rosicrucian Order Crotona Fellowship. We will be looking at this in more detail in Chapter 6. Gerald was interested enough to go to a play, *Pythagoras*, that was being put on in the theatre. He also started going to meetings of the Order. Bracelin takes up the story:

Now, at meetings, Gardner had noticed a group of people apart from the rest. They seemed rather brow-beaten by the others, kept themselves to themselves. They were the most interesting element, however. Unlike many of the others, they had to earn their livings, were cheerful and optimistic and had a real interest in the occult. They had

---

4 ibid.

carefully read many books on the subject: Unlike the general mass, who were supposed to have read all but seemed to know nothing.

Gardner always felt at home with them, was invited to their houses, and had many talks with them. The day came when one said:

"I have seen you before". Gardner, interested, asked where. "In a former life". Then all gathered around and agreed that this was so. What made it all remarkable to Gardner was that one of the number proceeded to describe a scene "exactly like one which I had written in A Goddess Arrives, which was due to be published any day then, and which in fact came out the following week".

Then someone said, "You belonged to us in the past - why don't you come back to us?"

"Now I was really very fond of them, and I knew that they had all sorts of magical beliefs" continues Gardner. "They had been very interested when I told them that an ancestress of mine had been burned alive as a witch at Newborough in Scotland ... And I would have gone through hell and high water even then for any of them.[5]

This group of people, whom Gerald calls "the most interesting element" are really some of the core individuals who feature in the pages of this book.

Bracelin continues:

He felt sure that they had some secret, there must be something which allowed them to take the slights at the theatre without really caring. He still thought that they might be mooting Yoga, or something of that nature. He asked them why they were in this community, and whether they believed what Aurelius [actually, Aureolis, the magical name of the head of the Fellowship, George Alexander Sullivan] had to offer. They explained that they

---

had been co-masons, and had followed Mabs (Mrs. Scott) when she had moved to this place; and added that they enjoyed the companionship.[6]

I explore later the story of the Co-Masons from Southampton and their relationship with Mabel Besant-Scott (Mabs).

To continue:

Gardner felt delighted that he was to be let into their secret. Thus it was that, a few days after the war had started, he was taken to a big house in the neighbourhood. This belonged to "Old Dorothy" - a lady of note in the district, "county" and very well-to-do. She invariably wore a pearl necklace, worth some £5,000 at the time.

It was in this house that he was initiated into witchcraft. He was very amused at first, when he was stripped naked and brought into a place "properly prepared" to undergo his initiation.

It was halfway through when the word Wica was first mentioned: "and I then knew that that which I had thought burnt out hundreds of years ago still survived".

"His first feeling about this was "How wonderful; to think that these things still survive", his interest as a folklorist stirred. Until then his opinion of witchcraft had been based upon the idea that witches killed for the purpose of gaining or raising power, and he had thought the persecutions of them fully justified. He found that his friends, after following Mabs to her settlement, had discovered an old Coven, and remained here because of that. "I found that Old Dorothy and some like her, plus a number of New Forest people, had kept the light shining. It was, I think, the most wonderful night of my life. In true witch fashion we had a dance afterwards, and kept it up until dawn".

For the first time he realised that witch-power came from within the body of the believer. He felt that all this should

[6] Bracelin p 165.

6

be generally known, and that if he could make his new knowledge available to all, objections to the cult would die down. But his request to be allowed to write about it all was turned down. No one was ever to know anything. The embargo was not lifted - and then only partially - until Dorothy died.[7]

2. Gerald Gardner in 1936.
The inscription reads "To Dafo with all Love, G B Gardner"

We will look in some detail at the individuals in the above account and at the circumstances surrounding Gerald Gardner's initiation. But first, let us explore the life of someone who was clearly very special to Gerald and who is integral to the whole existence of 'the witch cult': a witch he called 'Dafo'.

---

[7]   Bracelin pp 165-166.

2

A Witch called Dafo

Don't you know what 'ther' means? My first mentor, Tony Wedd, quoted Christopher Robin in A. A. Milne's *Winnie-the-Pooh* when attempting to explain the significance of the word 'the' in relation to those who talk about 'the Bible'.[1]

The basic meaning, of course, is that there's only one of whatever it is. And this is of particular significance when considering Gerald Gardner's repeated use of the phrase "the Witch" in his correspondence with Cecil Williamson in 1951:

> *I saw the Witch's daughter the other day.*[2]

> *... the Witch wants me down to talk to the Coven ...* [3]

> *... the Witch is sending a Car to fetch me on Tuesdy, so I have to go down + sweeten the Coven ...* [4]

We shall examine the context of these statements in due course. For the present purpose it is sufficient to note that there was one witch who was far more significant to Gardner than any other so that he called her 'the Witch', although mention of 'the Coven' implies that there were others around.

In an interview with Gerald Gardner, the *Daily Mirror* journalist, Marjorie Proops (1911-1996), wrote in 1957: *... twenty years ago, he met a girl witch named Dafo and that was it. Dafo brought out the occult in Gerald.*[5]

---

[1] A. A. Milne *Winnie-the-Pooh* (Methuen, 1926) p. 1.
[2] Boscastle Museum of Witchcraft Doc 42 - June 1951.
[3] ibid.
[4] Boscastle Museum of Witchcraft Doc 46 - August 1951.
[5] Marjorie Proops I Got the Low-down on this Witch Lark *Daily Mirror*, 10 April 1957.

The evidence which I shall give below strongly suggests that 'the Witch' was Edith Rose Woodford-Grimes, a teacher of elocution living in Highcliffe-on-Sea, Hampshire.

The existence of a witch called Dafo has long been mentioned in witchcraft circles. One of the earliest references to her that I have found is in the introduction to June Johns' book *King of the Witches*, published in 1969: *Gardner was initiated into the first grade of the cult by a witch called 'Daffo' in the New Forest ...*[6]

This is interesting, not just in attributing Gardner's initiation to her, but that Johns spells the name Daffo with a double 'f', which is what one might do if one had heard the name rather than seen it written down. It has been assumed that this was her witch name, but Edith's grandson told me that her nickname in the family had been 'Daff' for as long as he could remember. My thinking now is that this was adapted to Dafo by Gardner, for his own reasons.

We know from the identifying features given by Doreen Valiente in her book *The Rebirth of Witchcraft*[7] that the witch who went by the name of Dafo was a teacher of music and elocution and that her daughter married a dentist.[8] In fact, two of these things are correct but I am told by Edith's grandson that she was never a teacher of music. However, this information, together with details given by Lois Bourne in her book *Dancing with Witches*[9] and with references by Cecil Williamson, who, with Gerald Gardner, started a museum of magic and witchcraft at Castletown on the Isle of Man in 1951, in one of the interviews he gave for *Talking Stick* magazine[10] is sufficient to identify her.

---

[6] June Johns *King of the Witches* (Peter Davies 1969) p. 15.
[7] Doreen Valiente *The Rebirth of Witchcraft* (Robert Hale, 1989).
[8] ibid. p. 38.
[9] Lois Bourne *Dancing with Witches* (Robert Hale, 1998).
[10] Gerald Gardner: An Interview with Cecil Williamson *Talking Stick* VIII, Autumn 1992.

So, let us look at Dafo's early life. Edith Rose Wray was born in Malton in Yorkshire in the house now known as 5 Mill Cottages, Sheep's Foot Hill, off Castlegate, on 18th December 1887. Her mother was Caroline Wray (formerly Harrison) (1865-1939) and her father was William Henry Wray (1864-1930), an implement maker at the local waterworks.

3. Edith Woodford-Grimes' birthplace - 5 Mill Cottages, Sheepfoot Hill, Malton, Yorkshire

Malton is half way between the city of York and the seaside resort of Scarborough. It is in the North Riding of Yorkshire, separated by the River Derwent from its twin town of Norton, which is in the East Riding. It lies between the chalk Yorkshire Wolds, the Jurassic Howardian Hills, and the Vale of Pickering, which was once a glacial lake.

Edith's ancestors appear to have lived in the North and East Ridings of Yorkshire for several generations.

Edith was the second eldest of seven children in the family.

Oldest was Arthur Henry Wray, born 12th December 1883. He served in the First World War in the 17th Army Auxiliary Horse Company of the Royal Army Service Corps. He died in 1948.

Carrie was born on 12th September 1889. She married Albert V. Blackburn in 1915 and died in York in 1959.

Violet Annie was born on 12th January 1891. She married Douglas Thomson on 10th September 1922, and died in Ryedale in 1950.

Albert was born in 1892 and in 1923 married Amy Gertrude Hutchinson (born 1900) from Bradbury, Sedgefield, Co. Durham.

Olive Mary was born 25th August 1898 and in 1927 married Amy's brother, John E Hutchinson, who was a butcher. She died in November 2000 in Basingstoke, Hampshire.

The youngest child in the family was Ethel. She was born on 23rd August 1902 and was christened Gertrude Ethel, although later in life she seemed to change her name to Ethel Rose, perhaps simply because she didn't like the name 'Gertrude', which may have seemed a bit old-fashioned by the 1920s. Anyway, in 1925 she married Samuel Allan Morley (1895-1960), who was a cartoonist for D.C. Thomson of Dundee, who published 'Beano' and 'Dandy' among other comics, being responsible for such features as 'Dolly Dimple', 'Keyhole Kate' and 'Nosey Parker'.

All of the family except Edith were still living in Yorkshire by 1940. Edith seems to have been the only one who by that time had settled out of the county.

As the oldest girl in the family, Edith would, I imagine, have had to look after her younger sisters and brother. This would probably have stood her in good stead for her future role as a lady's maid and perhaps amplified her tendency to be somewhat snobbish and critical of others in later life.

A footnote to the entry for Edith in Wikipedia states:

> ... her grandfather, William Wray, was a Primitive Methodist preacher. Edith and her siblings received early education in a school run by the Primitive Methodist Church of Malton. Each year scholarships were provided for chosen students. Edith had a teacher who felt she had

tremendous potential and pursued opportunities for
further education. Edith won a scholarship through the
Primitive Methodist church of Malton.[11]

I have so far been unable to find out where Edith had her sec-
ondary education. The town of Malton did not at that time have
adequate facilities, so she probably had to go to York, travelling
every day the twenty miles or so by train. She certainly seems to
have been well educated, particularly in subjects such as English
language and literature, foreign languages, and drama. As she became better educated, she may have felt that an education
involved being able to "speak proper" and probably changed her
accent accordingly.

As part of my researches, I had tracked down her birth record and
sent for a copy of her birth certificate from the Ryedale District
registrar, whose area covers Malton. It turned out that Edith was
the Superintendent Registrar's great aunt and that she had a
photograph of Edith which she very kindly lent me. It is this
kind of coincidence which keeps one going! She also told me that
Edith was the adventurous sort, the only one of the family who
went away at the earliest opportunity, possibly to Harrogate.[12]

We don't come across Edith again until April 1911, when she was
23 years old. In the census taken that month, she is shown as a
lady's maid to Ethel Sarah Waud, who lived at Ferniehurst, a
large mansion situated roughly half way between the village of
Baildon, near Bradford, and the nearby town of Shipley, in the
West Riding of Yorkshire.

The family consisted of George Camille Waud (1869-1932), age 41,
an industrialist who owned the Britannia Mills in Bradford and

---

[11] Wikipedia entry for Edith Woodford-Grimes - footnote 3 [family lore, interview with
her first cousin, twice removed].
[12] Telephone conversation Ann Cook with the author 22 June 1998.

who was described on the census as a mohair spinner; his wife, Ethel Sarah Waud, age 40; and their daughter, Noreen Marjorie Waud, aged 10. There were eight domestic servants listed as living at Ferniehurst, though there may well have been others who lived in the surrounding area but who came in to work. Those listed were an Irish governess for Noreen; a butler; a footman; a cook; two housemaids and a kitchen maid, as well as Edith, the lady's maid.

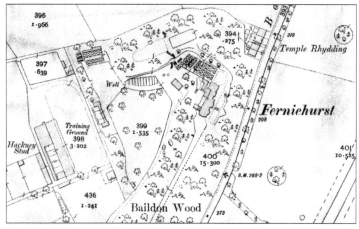

4. Ferniehurst and grounds, Baildon
(Reproduced from the 1906 Ordnance Survey map)

It is likely that Edith's educational background, plus her likely experience of all sorts of domestic duties while growing up, opened up the possibility of being appointed to that position, for a lady's maid was the personal attendant of the lady of the house and would be second only in rank to the housekeeper. One account gives some idea of a lady's maid's duties:

> *She must understand hair-dressing, dressmaking, packing, arranging the toilets for dinner parties, balls, etc. etc., must be possessed of good taste, must understand the care of dresses, boots, shoes, gloves, hats, bonnets, and the thorough art of repairing all clothes. She must be honest, quick, willing, clean, tidy and methodical, patient and contented ... [She] expects various perquisites: her*

mistress's discarded dresses, bonnets, mantles, jackets, and so on, and does as little as possible of the more menial work of her situation, giving herself too often "airs", as the saying is.[13]

From what I have learned of Edith in later life, I think it likely that she did indeed "give herself airs"! Ladies' maids have been described as the 'crème de la crème':

... she was responsible for her mistress' clothes, hair and overall appearance and comfort. ... she was a cut above the usual serving girl. She was required to be genteel as well as accomplished in the finer arts of style. She was often privy to the thoughts and feelings of her mistress, and close relationships were common. For this she was rewarded with first choice of her mistress' discarded clothing.[14]

Baildon, on the edge of the Pennine moors, has been settled since the Bronze Age and there are numerous cup-and-ring marks carved in the rock of nearby Baildon Moor. It was also a gathering point for the Gypsy community. Annual gatherings were said to date back to 1770, but by the time Edith was at Ferniehurst, the practice had died out.

Ferniehurst had been built between 1862 and 1863 for Edward, the youngest son of the industrialist, Sir Titus Salt, who had established a mill and village for his workers at nearby Saltaire, less than a mile away.

The building plans for Ferniehurst (probably named after Ferniehurst Castle in the Scottish borders) have been lost and there are no known photographs of the house, now demolished. It is thought by some, however, that it was similar in appearance to Milner Field, also near Baildon, built for Titus Salt, Jnr at about the same time.

---

[13] A. G. F. Eliot James *Our Servants, their duties to us and ours to them* (Ward Lock, 1883).

[14] https://www.janeausten.co.uk/the-assistance-of-servants.

Both Ferniehurst and Milner Field *came to epitomise the wealth and social pre-eminence of the Salt family.*[15]

An idea of what the house looked like and consisted of can be obtained from the catalogue which accompanied the auction sale of 1893, which was occasioned for financial reasons. Lee-Van den Daele and Beale describe Ferniehurst as follows:

> *... a mansion house with a drawing room, library, dining room, butler's pantry, twelve bedrooms, a tower, a billiard room which had a separate staircase and a large lavatory adjoining and the house also had accommodation for servants, including a servants' hall. ... There were also two bathrooms, (one with WC) and two housemaids' rooms with WCs. The residence was efficiently heated by coils and piping from the greenhouse boiler. ... [The] house was built from stone quarried on the site and the interior decoration had been carried out at great cost, with the drawing room decorated by Mr J. Aldam Heaton at a cost of over £1,000. There were also numerous outbuildings including a carriage house with space for six carriages, a separate laundry and there was even a model farm with standing room for cattle, piggeries, a bacon curing room, a tiled dairy, and poultry and pigeon houses. ... There were pleasure grounds round the house which were described as tastefully disposed and planted with forest trees, herbaceous, alpine plants, shrubs, and ferns of all descriptions. They included flower and kitchen gardens, several greenhouses and forcing pits, three vineries, a mushroom house and a gardener's bothy. There were also large soft and hard tennis grounds. The house itself was situated in an elevated position with a southeast aspect and it would have had magnificent views across the valley to Thackley and Wrose. According to the sale catalogue "the situation is unique and although in such close proximity to manufactories it enjoys an immunity from all nuisances including smoke.[16]*

---

[15] Richard Lee-Van den Daele and R David Beale *Milner Field: The Lost Country House of Titus Salt Jnr* (Barleybrook, 2013).

[16] ibid. pp. 163-165

After a delay of some three years, the house was acquired by George Camille Waud, who became a substantial figure in the local community, becoming Chairman of Baildon Urban District Council in the years 1899 to 1901.

Lee-Van den Daele and Beale state that he:

> ... was a partner in the firm of Christopher Waud and Co., mohair and alpaca spinners and had entered the mills as a young man and later joined his father, Mr. George Motley Waud, in control of the firm. In his leisure time he was a breeder of hackney horses [which are horses or ponies suitable for ordinary riding, particularly those "having a gait characterised by pronounced flexion of the knee"] and in 1899 he built a hackney training ground and stud at the back of Ferniehurst on what was to become the site of Ferniehurst School.

> He was also said to be of a very philanthropic nature and to have greatly helped the poor of Baildon.[17]

There was a mischievous side to George Waud, as the *Shipley Times and Express* reported:

> Apropos of the scare created by numerous reports about German airships having been seen hovering over this country lately, Mr. George C. Waud, of Ferniehurst, Baildon, who loves a practical joke as much as anyone, tells a good story. It will be remembered that during the great religious revival in North Wales, occasioned by the preaching of Evan Roberts, the newspapers gave considerable prominence to what were announced as "Mysterious Lights". Mr Waud now confesses that he was the culprit. "I was staying at my place in Wales when feeling was at its highest," he writes. "All sorts of visitations were announced. My house was beautifully situated for the joke, so I had several black paper fire balloons specially made, and I used to float them off, according to the wind, with a large cotton waste trailer soaked in paraffin. All the

---

17 ibid. p. 168.

local and Liverpool papers were full of these 'mysterious lights' for some time until I wrote to one of the papers and explained the hoax.[18]

Lee-Van den Daele and Beale continue:

Also a great rose grower, he was prominently connected with Saltaire Rose Show; indeed, he and Father O'Sullivan of Shipley were said to have one of the rarest collections of roses in the country.[19]

Indeed, George had a rose named after him, a hybrid tea, deep rose pink, double flowers with a good old rose scent. The rose, George C Waud, was introduced by Alex Dickson and Sons in 1908. It is described as:

Flower cochineal carmine tinted vermilion and orange, large, very full, high-centred, generally single on long stiff stems, very sweet. Growth robust, erect, free-flowering.[20]

The rose was even the subject of a cigarette card, featuring in the 1913 series of Wills's cigarette cards (No. 85). The card has a fine coloured illustration of the rose, and the reverse gives certain additional details:

The colour of this rose is quite unique, and, unlike many of a similar nature, it does not fade. It is free flowering and vigorous, and the flowers are large, full and perfectly formed, with high pointed centre, making it an excellent exhibition variety. Introduced in 1908, and awarded the Gold Medal of the National Rose Society.

In later life Edith was obsessed with roses and her garden was full of them. Could her interest have been ignited by her employer's enthusiasm? And did she, along with her other duties, find time to help him with their cultivation?

---

[18] *Shipley Times and Express* 7 March 1913.
[19] Lee-Van den Daele and Beale p. 168.
[20] T. Geoffrey W Henslow, MA, FRHS *The Rose Encyclopedia* (Vickery, Kyle and Co. Ltd., 1922).

5. Edith in her younger days

6. Edith, again, in her younger days

In the late 1920s Edith was a tutor in drama and English literature and I think it likely that her interest in such subjects and education in general dated back to the time when she gained a scholarship at the age of 11. Such topics as drama and English literature would almost certainly form part of her school curriculum. Edith obviously had, or developed, an enthusiasm, probably for education in general and, after she left school, would have taken the opportunity to educate herself through such things as the local library and any day or evening classes that may have been arranged.

Baildon was an ideal place in many ways for an educated woman like Edith to thrive. It was within easy reach of such urban centres as Bradford and Leeds, both of which had a strong adult education tradition, with workers' evening classes. In her evenings and days off, Edith could have walked or cycled to Shipley station, just a mile away from Ferniehurst, to take the train into Bradford.

In addition, a new Ladies' Teacher Training College opened in 1911 in the neighbouring village of Bingley, only some three miles away from Ferniehurst and thus within easy reach on foot or by bicycle for Edith to attend the numerous extra-mural activities that were on offer. The College's first intake of students was 102 women from in and around the West Riding of Yorkshire. In view of her future teaching posts, it is interesting to speculate whether Edith enrolled at the College. However, her Teachers' Registration Council record from 1940 does not show any formal qualification from that institution, but I would be most surprised if she did not take advantage of the activities that went on there.

The principal of the college was Helen Wodehouse (1880-1964), who went on to be Professor of Education at the University of Bristol, one of only a very few female professors. Unusually at the time, she rejected Christianity but remained naturally religious. She is described as being inspirational, and it is quite possible that she influenced Edith by her extra-mural lectures, perhaps encouraging an attitude of challenging orthodoxy.

As lady's maid to Ethel Waud, Edith would in all likelihood have had the opportunity to meet some of the more affluent and influential residents of Baildon and the surrounding area. We do not know where she first acquired an interest in esoteric matters, but it is no exaggeration to say that she was living in the very best village in the whole of the northern half of England to enable her to come into contact with former members of the most famous occult revival organisation of the late 19th and early 20th Centuries: the Hermetic Order of the Golden Dawn.

The Hermetic Order of the Golden Dawn was founded in 1888. The story of its foundation is that Rev. A.F.A. Woodford, a member of the Societas Rosicruciana in Anglia (S.R.I.A.), a masonic Rosicrucian society, found some old documents which gave details of rituals which seemed to be Rosicrucian in character and to originate in Germany. He gave these to Dr William Wynn Westcott, who then approached two other members of the S.R.I.A., Dr W.R. Woodman and Samuel Liddell Mathers. They managed to contact a German woman named Anna Sprengel who authorised them to form an Order in England to be known as the Golden Dawn.

It is now generally considered that Mathers and Woodman were taken in by the documents, which were likely forgeries, and that Anna Sprengel never existed. However, the Golden Dawn philosophy and practices are substantially rooted in what has been called the Western Mystery Tradition as opposed to the Eastern traditions which were in large part the inspiration for Madame Blavatsky's Theosophy.

Most modern magical orders owe something, and probably a great deal, to the Golden Dawn, for example its subdivision into ten degrees. The name "Golden Dawn" strictly related only to the Outer Order made up of the lower degrees. The higher degrees constituted the Inner Order of the Rosae Rubae et Aureae Crucis.

Following the inception of the Golden Dawn, the Isis-Urania Temple was established in London in 1888; the Osiris Temple in Weston-super-Mare and the Horus Temple in Bradford were established in the same year. The only other temples were the Amen-Ra Temple in Edinburgh (established 1893) and the Ahathoor Temple in Paris (established 1894).

The Horus Temple was the only one in the whole of the North and Midlands of England. R.A. Gilbert writes that:

> The Horus Temple was the brainchild of T.H. Pattinson
> (Vota vita mea), a watchmaker of Baildon ... It soon

*became an active temple and by the end of 1896 ... it had
acquired 54 members (40 men and 14 women).²¹*

As well as Pattinson, eight other members of the Temple lived in
Baildon, which, as a village of only some 6,000 inhabitants in the
1911 Census, had therefore by far the largest concentration of
members (9 out of 54).²²

Thomas Henry Pattinson was the Imperator of the Horus Temple
and also a prominent member of the Societas Rosicruciana in Anglia. His wife, Eliza, was also a member of the Golden Dawn. He
lived at 20 Westfield Terrace, Baildon. Next door, at 19 Westfield
Terrace, lived another Golden Dawn member, Francis Drake Harrison.

Other Golden Dawn members living in Baildon included Oliver
Firth and Florence Margaret Spink, 8 Rushcroft; John Midgeley,
35 East Parade; Catherine Elizabeth Spink, Baildon Lodge; Robert
Elliott Steele, Hawthorne House; and Gertrude Jane Spink,
Hawkswood. The three Spink women were probably related and
some of their houses, particularly Baildon Lodge, were quite substantial.

The heyday of the Horus Temple was in the 1890s, but even when
Edith was at Ferniehurst there were still some former Golden
Dawn members living in Baildon.

I do not know whether Edith had come into contact with Co-Masonry before she moved south from Baildon. I have been told²³
that there were Co-Masons amongst the Theosophical Society
lodge in Bradford, which had been founded by old members of the
Bradford Horus Temple of the Golden Dawn. If that is the case,
then it is at least possible that Edith was exposed to Co-Masonry
while she was at Baildon.

²¹ R. A. Gilbert *The Golden Dawn Companion* (Aquarian, 1986) p. 35.
²² ibid. pp. 35-37 and 133-138.
²³ Telephone conversation between Chris Lycett and the author 8 June 1998.

Baildon seems to have been just the sort of place where occult and esoteric activity flourished, and there appears to have been quite an overlap of membership between the various esoteric groups.

Apart from the Golden Dawn, the other major organisation of that sort at the turn of the 20th Century was the Theosophical Society. This had been founded in 1875 by Helena Blavatsky, a Russian occultist and esoteric teacher. It had as its objectives:

1 - To form a nucleus of the universal brotherhood of humanity without distinction of race, creed, sex, caste, or colour.

2 - To encourage the study of comparative religion, philosophy and science.

3 - To investigate the unexplained laws of nature and the powers latent in man.

Theosophy is concerned with the evolution of the universe, both physical and non-physical, and incorporates wisdom from both East and West in its teachings and practices, including the acknowledgement of reincarnation as a natural process and the application of universal laws.

Although the Society started in New York, Theosophy spread rapidly to England and branches were formed in various places.

There had been a Theosophical Lodge in nearby Bradford since 1891, one of the earliest in England. By 1910: A Lodge at Baildon was commenced after a series of public lectures had been given by Miss Pattinson, W. Gush and J. Midgley.[24] Miss Pattinson was probably Thomas Pattinson's daughter, and John Midgley had been a Golden Dawn member living in Baildon.

I think it highly likely that, even if she had not previously made contact, Edith would have attended these public lectures and been sufficiently attracted to Theosophical ideas to have become

---

[24] History of the Theosophical Movement in Bradford (1891-1941) - www.ts-bradford.org.uk/theosoc/btshisto.htm

a member of the group which met regularly, probably in Pattinson's house or workshop.

At some stage the group became a Lodge and started to hold regular public meetings. Certainly by the time the First World War started, in August 1914, there were regular weekly Sunday evening meetings of the Lodge, including lectures from visiting speakers, held at the Mechanics' Institute in the village.

Topics such as 'Reincarnation', 'the Human Aura', 'Invisible Helpers', and 'Body, Soul and Spirit' were among those featured. Speakers were mostly members of the local Lodge, including Miss Pattinson and John Midgley, but also from the nearby Bradford Lodge.

It is total speculation on my part, but I think that, as part of her rise in status by becoming a lady's maid, Edith may have, at least informally, taken on a new name. And, I think, as is often the case, the surname that she took on was her mother's maiden name, Harrison. I think it possible that Edith may have become quite involved in the local Theosophical group, have got to know Francis Drake Harrison and his family, and, taking the coincidence of names into account, in an attempt to carve out a new life and personality for herself, had adopted, informally, the surname of 'Harrison'. (Though, I could, of course, be completely wrong!) It is perhaps more likely as Francis Drake Harrison had not just been a member of the Golden Dawn, but of the Theosophical Society as well. Also by this time Edith may have become interested in numerology, which may have had an influence. There is a "Miss E. Harrison" in the list of members.

We do not know how long Edith worked for the Wauds, just that she was in the Bournemouth area, at least for a holiday, in 1917, and was living in Southampton after she got married in 1920.

The event which I suspect precipitated any such change was, of course, the First World War (1914-1918). Southampton and the surrounding area was one of the main recipients of the hospital ships which were ferrying the injured over from France. With most of the young men joining up, it was only natural for the young women in the caring professions, such as Edith, to give what help they could. And her employers would probably have encouraged such patriotic activity.

The main organisation to which such young women might be drawn towards was known as the Voluntary Aid Detachment (V.A.D.). It had been formed in 1909 by the Red Cross and the Order of St. John but expanded greatly as the war progressed. Essentially, it provided nursing services, both in France and at home. A contemporary advertisement states that *nursing members, cooks, kitchen-maids, clerks, house-maids, ward-maids, laundresses, motor-drivers, etc. are urgently needed.*

However, I could find no Edith Rose Wray in the records kept by the Red Cross of all the V.A.D.s. I was puzzled for some time and then it occurred to me that perhaps for some reason she had maintained her change of name. This was quite a bit easier to accomplish in those days than it would be today.

Certainly she did it in more recent times. For example, Gerald Gardner, for his own reasons in financial dealings involving the Fiveacres Club, refers to Edith, as a supposed financial backer, as 'Elsie'. And Doreen Valiente told me that Edith was introduced to her as Elsie.[25]

But no 'Elsie Wray' appeared likely. So, working on the assumption that she may indeed have adopted the surname of Harrison, I looked up 'Elsie Harrison'.

There were four entries for 'Miss Elsie Harrison'. Three were in other parts of the country, but, looking at the fourth one, I felt

---

[25] Letter Doreen Valiente to the author 24 August 1998.

reasonably sure I had found her. At least, I think it's likely, because her address is given as 1 Home Cottage, Highcliffe-on-Sea, Hants., which is now on Rothesay Drive and is within the grounds of Highcliffe Castle. This fact alone led me to think I was on to something, as Highcliffe was the village where the witch cult was subsequently brought into being.

7. Edith in 1917

Elsie Harrison worked as a V.A.D. from 27th May 1917 to 30th September 1918. She was engaged as a "Second Parlourmaid" at £34 per annum. She was employed at the Red Cross Auxiliary Hospital for Officers at Branksome Gate, Bournemouth and was in Lady Dudley's Department, Bournemouth Hospitals.

The month before she started work at the hospital, Edith had a photograph taken by W. Hazel, professional photographer of 116 Old Christchurch Road, Bournemouth. Remembering that one of the 'perks' of a ladies' maid was to be given her lady's cast-off clothes, one can see that her coat is somewhat military, which was very fashionable at the time.[26]

It is total speculation on my part, but I suspect that Edith's decision to leave her employment at Ferniehurst and to seek a nursing post with the Red Cross may have been due to the loss of a lover, killed in action, as was the experience of so many women during the Great War.

——————————•—————•◆—————••——————————

On 16th June 1920, Edith married Samuel William Woodford Grimes in the parish church of St Leonard, Malton.

Samuel was born on 12th September 1880 to Samuel and Kate Grimes in Bangalore, India. In the Great War he had been a Sergeant in the King's Own Scottish Borderers and a Warrant Officer, Class 2 in the Royal Engineers and the Royal Scots Fusiliers. At the time of his marriage to Edith he was living in Southampton and was a clerk in the local War Pensions Office.

Edith was 32 years of age. Because of the ravages of the war, suitable men were in short supply, and if Edith was intending to have a child, she would need to find a husband without delay. I have been told by someone who knew Edith well that it was never much of a marriage. Perhaps her choice was not wise or at any rate taken in haste.

---

[26] I was told this by Daru Rooke, Museum Manager at Bradford City Council.

8. Samuel William Woodford Grimes

Edith and Samuel moved into Denton Cottage, 67 Osborne Road, Portswood, a suburb of Southampton, probably immediately following their marriage in 1920 and certainly before Rosanne, their first and only child, was born, on 30th June 1921, in Edith's parents' house in Malton. Was this because she wanted to be near her mother at the time of such a life-changing event, or merely that, by being born in Yorkshire, the child would be eligible to play cricket for that county?

For the next three years, Edith was undoubtedly kept busy looking after Rosanne and carrying out general household duties, but by 1924, Rosanne was probably old enough to allow Edith to pursue other interests.

Edith had in all likelihood discovered that she had a natural aptitude for English and drama while she was at school and, though we don't know for certain, it seems likely that she pursued these interests while she was at Ferniehurst.

Starting in 1924, Edith became a tutor in English and dramatic literature to various student groups authorised by the Workers Educational Association and the Extra-Mural Department of University College, Southampton.[27]

At that stage, it would appear that she had no formal qualification, and it is likely that this would probably have involved teaching evening classes which could be fitted in with her domestic duties.

From 1930 to 1934, Edith attended vacation courses organised by the London Academy of Music. This had been founded in 1861 and was originally established to provide training and examination in music. However, it soon expanded its activities to include spoken English, which seems to have been Edith's particular interest, resulting in her being awarded a Teacher's Diploma as an Associate in Elocution (A.L.A.M.).

This would seem to suggest that Edith had specialised in training in elocution. I think probably at the back of her mind was the idea that there would be sufficient demand for elocution practice for her to set up eventually as an elocution teacher privately.

The 1920s was a period when there was still a disparagement of regional accents and a feeling that for individuals to make progress in the world, they needed to 'talk proper'. It is, of course, the subject of G.B. Shaw's play, *Pygmalion*, first performed in 1914.

---

[27] Teachers Registration Council Register Entry no. 96621 dated August 1940.

But for Edith, elocution was far more than just accent. For her, it was all tied up with self-expression, and I think it is significant that from 1928 onwards she always described herself as a 'Teacher of Elocution and Dramatic Art', both for the Southampton Education Authority Evening Institutes and privately.

Indeed, she may have been influenced by Elsie Fogerty (1865-1945) who:

> ... was an English teacher who bravely departed from the customary practice of "voice and diction" also called elocution. At that time "Voice and Diction" focused entirely on the mouth and nasal cavity to produce speech sounds. Fogerty's technique ended up focusing on the entire body and voice to produce speech. At first, she used just the lungs to resonate the sound, but soon included the whole body, because she discovered that posture and movement also affected speech. It ultimately became known as the "Body and Voice" technique. And, it can be rightly said, she 'taught the stage to speak'.[28]

In 1906 Elsie Fogerty founded the Central School of Speech-Training and Dramatic Arts (now the Central School of Speech and Drama). Whether Edith attended any of her training courses, I do not know, though she was certainly influenced by her. Indeed, one wonders whether Edith's choice of the pseudonym "Elsie" was made out of respect for Elsie Fogerty.

We do not know at what stage Edith took up her esoteric interests after settling in Southampton, but, as we will see in the next chapter, she is highly likely to have made contact with members of a remarkable family - the Masons - particularly after they came to live in a house in the same street as Edith in 1922.

---

[28] Wikipedia entry - Elsie Fogerty.

But, before we look at the Mason family, I am going to jump forward to the 1950s and 1960s, when Edith was a mature woman and living in Highcliffe-on-Sea, because I have had the good fortune to have been given some vivid accounts by those who knew her, including her grandson and neighbours.

Edith's grandson, Keith, was born during the war. His mother, Rosanne, was involved with war work so he was largely brought up by his grandmother. His impression of her was that she was very Victorian and correct. She was well-dressed and elegant and always had good quality clothes. Indeed, she had a tendency to 'look down her nose' at most people, often to the embarrassment of the family.

9. Edith in the 1950s

In 1960, after Gerald Gardner's wife, Donna, had died, Lois Bourne went up to the Isle of Man, where he was living, to help him at a vulnerable time:

> *During my stay on the island, Gerald asked me if I would help him sort through his papers and documents, so that he could decide what should be kept for reference and what could be disposed of. It was necessary that I should read these to him, and whilst doing so, I came across correspondence from a lady called Mrs. Woodford Grimes. She wrote in a very stern manner, castigating him for his blatant publicity tendencies, warning him about the deplorable people he became involved with, and casting aspersions on the motives of his converts. I recall that he was a little embarrassed by the letter but dismissive of it and said 'She is old and has become crabby!'*[29]

One wonders whether this attitude originated from her role as a lady's maid back in Baildon. Certainly this could be the origin of her reputation for being good at dressmaking and 'making and mending' generally. Also, Keith told me that she had been a J.P. (Justice of the Peace), in other words, a magistrate.

She taught Keith how to darn his own socks, which was very useful when he went into the army. Indeed, she was always cooking and baking. Keith remembers particularly her marmalade tarts.

Edith made a reasonable income from her teaching of elocution. One neighbour said:

> *I went to Mrs-Woodford Grimes because I had a slight speech impediment. I lisped. She taught me how to get rid of it. She was a very nice lady and a very good elocution teacher.*

> *Her house was a bit creepy, lots of dark wood, lots of ornaments and a grandfather clock that struck. But once you had gone through to the sun lounge it was light - lots*

---

[29] Lois Bourne, op. cit. p. 58.

of windows looking out onto the garden, which was rather overgrown with roses.[30]

Another said:

I have a picture in my mind of Mrs. Woodford-Grimes as a classic little old lady - slightly plump, a lot of grey hair in a bun and a shawl around her shoulders. As a girl I was shy and had a mild stutter and Mrs Woodford-Grimes helped me in that regard. I also needed extra help with my schoolwork. She particularly helped me with literature - and that was a very rich experience. I only went into her front room - or occasionally into her kitchen if she was making a cup of tea. Her house seemed dark - it was not sunlit. I would say it was creepy but not frightening.[31]

There was, nevertheless, a certain fear or apprehension of her:

If ever one of our footballs or cricket balls or one of my model planes went over into Mrs Woodford-Grimes' garden we never got them back. I was too terrified to ask for them. She must have had loads of our balls!

Her land was L-shaped so part of it was over the wall at the bottom of our garden. I remember once - when I was about seven or eight - climbing over to get a model plane that had gone over, because I thought she would not see me. I threw the plane back and as I was scrambling back over the wall I heard her shouting at me.

Her garden had roses and roses and roses everywhere, with concrete pathways in between. She didn't seem to be friendly with people in Avenue Road. She never socialised. Often I would see her sitting in her rocking chair in the bay window of the house, looking out on to Avenue Road.[32]

---

[30] "BC" interview with Ian Stevenson 17 July 2003.
[31] "NC" interview with Ian Stevenson 17 July 2003.
[32] "JC" interview with Ian Stevenson 17 July 2003.

10. Avenue Cottage, Edith's home from 1940 to 1975

Edith also had a black cat called Jimmy:

> *I liked* [him]. *I used to pick him up and stroke him, but sometimes he'd scratch. The really weird thing is that when I took my husband to see our old house the other day a cat with exactly the same coat as Jimmy - black but tinged with reddy brown - ran out. I said "Jimmy" and it just stood and looked at me. Now that's spooky.*[33]

> *Now I love cats - we had one at home. But Jimmy used to terrify me. He loved to come into our house and get up into the attic. But I tried to keep him out. If ever he got into our house I used to have nightmares. In the nightmares Jimmy would appear larger than life at the top of the stairs.*[34]

Keith remembers that there was a lot of books around in the house and there was a large bookcase. There were definitely some books on witchcraft, some of which have been passed down in the family.

Edith was clearly a central figure in what Gerald Gardner referred to as the witch cult, and we shall look at her relationship with him in more detail in a later chapter. But for the moment let us now turn our attention to the Mason family.

---

[33] "BC" interview with Ian Stevenson 17 July 2003.
[34] "JC" interview with Ian Stevenson 17 July 2003.

3
Masons in more ways than one

In 1922 Edith became aware that a family sharing some of her interests had moved in to a large early Victorian semi-detached house in the same street. The house, no. 1 Osborne Road, was known as 'Beechwood', probably because of the large beech trees in the grounds. The family living there were the Masons. As Edith would soon discover, they were Masons in more than just name. They were in many ways a remarkable family.

So, who were the Mason family? They seem to have been based in and around the Southampton area for at least 150 years. Let us start, somewhat arbitrarily, with Job Mason (1809-1866). He was born in the small town of Romsey, some seven miles inland from Southampton. In his youth he seems to have been a petty thief, being fined 45 shillings in 1830 for stealing cabbage plants from a garden, and in the same year imprisoned for stealing shoemakers' lasts.

The most interesting offence, however, was at the age of 18 when he was fined 10 shillings for letting off fireworks on 5th November 1827. Why it should be an offence to let off fireworks on Guy Fawkes Night, a day traditionally associated with such activities, I do not know. Perhaps he let them off where he wasn't supposed to, or perhaps he had made them himself and they were not considered safe. In any case, he was not the only member of the Mason family to be involved in chemical concoctions or to be imprisoned, as we shall see. But it is perhaps the first indication that the family as a whole were, to say the least, unusual, and even unconventional, in their activities.

Job's son, William, was born in 1831 and, by 1851, was employed in Romsey as a chair maker or, more precisely, as a "chair bottomer". In 1860 he married Mary Workman from Monmouth, in Wales, and by the following year they were living in Southampton and William had added umbrella-making to his chair making. With the sort of climate that southern England enjoys, the trade of umbrella-making would be likely to flourish, which it certainly seemed to in the Masons' case.

It seemed to be very much a matter of the assembly of ready-made components, probably in one room of the family home. The invention of steel ribs by Samuel Fox in the middle of the 19th Century would have encouraged this process.

11. George Miles Mason

On 3rd February, William's third child, George Miles Mason (1860-1938), was born at 19 Winchester Street in Southampton. His middle name, Miles, comes from his maternal grandfather, but may also have been inspired by George Miles Mason, a well-known potter of the early 19th Century from Stoke-on-Trent. By 1881, George and his sister, Kate, were established in the family business of umbrella making on the Isle of Wight, at 111 High Street, Ryde.

12. Rosetta Toms

On 20th May that year, George married Rosetta Toms (1861-1943), a servant girl working in Southampton. Rosetta's parents were Mary Ann and William Toms, who lived in Landport, a settlement on the edge of Portsmouth. At the time of Rosetta's birth William was a seaman on *H.M.S. Excellent.* Probably most of the people living in the Portsmouth area, certainly at that time, had some connection with the Royal Navy or the naval dockyard. William had been born in Portsmouth in 1827 and his wife had been born in Gosport, over the other side of Portsmouth Harbour, in the same year. By the age of 54, William's sailing days were over, but he was still working for the Royal Navy, this time as a labourer in the dockyards.

13. The New Forest and surrounding area

George and Rosetta's first child, Susie Mary, was born in Ryde on 22nd August 1882. 'Susie' was the name given on her birth certificate, not Susan. Perhaps again a glimpse of something slightly unorthodox, or it may simply have the same origin as marine painter, Harry Hudson Rodmell's first name: his father decided that it was pointless naming him 'Henry' since everyone would call him 'Harry' anyway![1]

On 1st September 1885, Ernest William Mason was born. We shall look at him and his life in a later chapter. By the previous year, the family had moved back to Southampton and George had added "photographer" to the family business of umbrella making. But by 1891, by which time his family were living at 3 South Front in central Southampton, he is shown on the Census returns as being a sculptor (artist). It is difficult to know whether he made a living from this: certainly he did not advertise in the street directories and Southampton City Art Gallery does not have any

[1] Arthur G Credland *Shipping Posters and Graphic Works: Harry Hudson Rodmell 1896-1984* (Hull City Museums and Hutton Press, 1999).

examples of his work. However, it seems as if he was able to make a good living from some source because by 1900 the family was established in 28 Dorset Street where they lived until 1921.

By 1901, George was firmly established as a photographic lantern slide maker and colourer. Susie and Ernest were similarly employed, and Rosetta, George's second daughter, is described as a slide painter.

14. Four generations of the Mason family. Standing: Ernie Mason, Susie Mason and Arthur Fudge. Seated: Rosetta Fudge, Rosetta Mason and Edna Fudge. The child is Judith Ann Fudge. Beechwood Hall, Osborne Road, Southampton - January 1935

In 1922, they moved into no. 1 Osborne Road, Portswood, and the following year we know that George was engaged in the business of lantern-slide manufacture, involving him in optics and photography, in which his wife, Rosetta, and son, Ernest, played an active part. They had a shop at 14 Carlton Place, Southampton. George was what one might call an inventor. He was also an astronomer, having constructed an observatory in the large garden attached to the house.

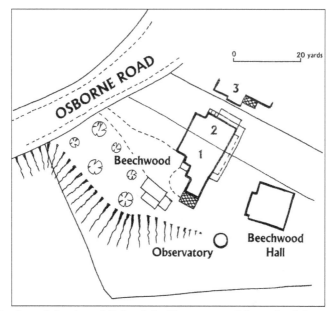

15. Beechwood, Beechwood Hall and the Observatory, 1 Osborne Road, Portswood, Southampton (based on the 1906 Ordnance Survey map)

This was the everyday, if somewhat unusual, side of the family. But there was another side - the esoteric, which linked anthroposophy, Theosophy, Co-Masonry, Rosicrucianism and witchcraft into a lively mix.

The oldest child, Susie Mary Mason, seems to have been the organiser of the family. She was indicated in the local directories as being the Hon. Secretary of the Southampton Lodge of the Theosophical Society from 1929 to 1934. This Lodge was in existence from at least 1915 since Ernie Mason had been a member from that date.[2] Susie joined the year after Ernie.

The Lodge seemed to thrive and, in November 1925, Annie Besant opened new lodge premises at 32 Carlton Crescent, Southampton. Susie was appointed a member of the House Sub-Committee that same year and, in 1927, took on the role of Book Steward. In

[2] Southampton Lodge Minute Books - Theosophical Society in England archives. I was able to consult these through the good offices of Leslie Price.

1928, she was elected a member of the Committee and was appointed Assistant Secretary, becoming Joint Secretary (presumably a promotion!) in 1929. By 1931, Susie was elected Secretary but by 1933 she was demoted to assistant secretary. By 1936, both she and her brother, Ernie, had resigned. I will recount the probable reason for this shortly.

16. Susie Mary Mason

During this time, Susie was living with her parents and brother at Beechwood. During the Second World War, she was an Air Raid Precautions officer and an ambulance driver.

Their sister, Rosie or Rose (Rosetta) Fudge, was also a member from 1924 to 1933. Named after her mother, Rosetta had married William James Fudge in 1903 and was living in St. Mary Street, Southampton, running a drapery business with him. She had been born in 1884 and was interested in Rudolf Steiner's anthroposophy, possessing a copy of the first of his books to be translated into English, dated 1910, in a limited edition of 1500 copies. By 1901 she was part of the family business as a slide painter.

To digress for a moment, on the house at 12 Pear Tree Road, Derby, there is a blue plaque reading "Alice Wheeldon, 1866-1919, Anti-war activist, socialist and suffragist, lived here behind her shop". Unlikely as it may seem, this has close links to the Mason family through Susie and Ernie's brother, Alfred George Mason, known as Alf. He could definitely be called eccentric although he had no known esoteric interests. Though perhaps he did, for his mother-in-law was a spiritualist and he could well have become interested, even if he hadn't been influenced by members of his own family. He is best known today for his supposed part in the so-called "plot to kill Lloyd George", which became the title of a book by Nicola Rippon.[3]

Alf was born at 3 South Front, Southampton on 13th October 1892 (the same day as my grandmother, Lottie Matilda Brown, who will feature in the scene at the beginning of Chapter 13). In 1908, at the age of 16, he was apprenticed to Martin's, a chemist in High Street, Southampton. At the age of 20, he moved to London, working as a chemist at Guy's Hospital Analytical Department. He was registered as a chemist and druggist by the Pharmaceutical Society of Great Britain the following year.

---

[3] Nicola Rippon *The Plot to Kill Lloyd George - The Story of Alice Wheeldon and the Pear Tree Conspiracy* (Wharncliffe Books, 2009).

In May 1915, at the age of 22, Alf married Winnie Wheeldon from Derby. She, and others in her family, were active in left-wing politics, Winnie being a pacifist and joining the No-Conscription Fellowship.

During this period, at the height of the First World War, conscientious objectors were interned, and the Wheeldons, probably encouraged by a government-planted spy and "agent provocateur", devised a plan to allow them to escape custody. Alf (or "Alph", as Winnie always called him!) was to put his skills in chemistry to bear in producing the necessary poison, which he did, namely strychnine and curare. He always claimed that this was to poison the dogs guarding the internees.

In January 1917, Alf, together with the Wheeldon family, was arrested and charged with plotting to murder Lloyd George. The case was tried at the Old Bailey in London and was said to be the first trial in English legal history to rely on the evidence of a secret agent.

They were all found guilty of conspiracy to murder. Alf was sentenced to seven years imprisonment. However, after two years, at the request of Lloyd George, they were allowed out on licence. Alf died on 20th June 1963.

As well as the plaque, which was erected in 2013, there is a play by Sheila Rowbotham entitled *The Friends of Alice Wheeldon*; and *The Eye in the Door* (1993), which is the second volume of the Regeneration trilogy by Pat Barker, about the affair.

And, in 2009, Nicola Rippon's was published.[4] It tells the whole story as far as it has yet been revealed, which seems to indicate that whilst the Wheeldons, with Alf's assistance, did plan to poison guard dogs at internment camps to help the escape of conscientious objectors, the supposed plot to kill the Prime Minister was based on casual words reported by a government infiltrator, and was a convenient issue with which to attack

---

4 ibid.

socialists, anarchists and pacifists. It is doubtful whether the case against the Wheeldons would have stood up in a present-day court of law. It is likely that they were deliberately set up and framed by the authorities who were worried about opposition to the war.

———————————— •·━◆━·• ————————————

To return south, the Mason family were familiar with the New Forest, which, at its nearest, was a mere six miles from their home in Southampton. The Forest will become important in our story, so it is of some significance that it was a familiar place for the Masons right back to the end of the 19th Century. All the family seemed to know the Forest and they used to take frequent cycle rides exploring the area.

At some stage before 1899, they got to know the Tame family of Bolderwood in Minstead parish in the heart of the New Forest. They are frequently mentioned in the diary of 17-year old Beatrice Ellen Tame for 1899, which has now been published.[5]

Beatrice refers to Mr. and Mrs. Mason and their son, Ernie, cycling over from Southampton to visit:

> *Saw Mr. Mason he is coming out when he can get a camera that he wants* [23 Apr] *Mr. Mason and Rosie cycled from Southampton this morning for the day. Rose is staying for a week* [12 May] *Dick rode Rosie's bicycle in, as Sue wants it* [19 May] *Mr. and Mrs. Mason arrived just before 12 o'clock after a windy ride. Mr. Mason went on at the trap, he is most kindly varnishing it and making it fresh and nice* [23 May] *Annie went in to Southampton, she rode her bicycle down to Lyndhurst and went in by train and had a tooth out ... Mrs. Mason and Ernie have come back with her, they have all bicycled, Ernie, all the way* [17 July] *The back tyre cover of Ernie's steed began to burst out by the*

---

5   Veronica Walton (ed.) *Beatrice of Bolderwood - The Diary of a New Forest Girl 1899* (New Forest Ninth Centenary Trust, 2004).

valve, so we let the air out and I bound it up and it bore him home. [23 July] *... we met Alf and Mrs. Mason and Alfie in the motor and Mr. Mason on his bicycle ...* [9 Sept]

So, Mr. and Mrs. Mason live in Southampton; they ride bicycles; Mr. Mason is concerned about getting the right camera; they have a son, Ernie, and Rosie/Rose, Sue and Alfie are also mentioned. They are Rosetta, Susie and Alf. In 1899 George was 39 and his wife Rosetta 38. Susie was 17, Rosetta 15, Ernie 14, and Alf 7.

The identity of the Masons referred to in Beatrice's diary as 'our' Mason family is confirmed in the 1901 Census, which includes, as a visitor to Bolderwood Lodge, Rose Mason, a slide painter. The manufacture of lantern slides was, of course, the family business.

We can therefore deduce that the Mason family, as a group and individually, used to make bicycling trips into the New Forest from Southampton, often staying with their friends, the Tames, at Bolderwood Lodge, which acted as a sort of informal bed and breakfast establishment.

And we can assume that they explored the Forest, both on bicycle and on foot. In this context it is interesting that Gerald Gardner told Doreen Valiente that one of the places that the witches met was in Mark Ash Wood, which is right next to Bolderwood Lodge. Its use for such purposes may have been initially because the Mason family got to know that locality well after visiting on a regular basis.

4
Ernie Mason - The Magus

Ernest William Mason, commonly known as "Ernie", is not just a figure from the archives. Fortunately, I made contact with someone who had not only known Ernie Mason but clearly felt that he was the most remarkable man he had ever met.

It is always good when the individuals who feature in this book were known to people who could give me first-hand experience of what those individuals were like. In other words, they were able to bring them to life. Penny Rudkin of Southampton Central Library, put me in touch with Bill Wakefield, a member of the Southampton Astronomical Society, who had known Ernie Mason well. I subsequently had several long telephone conversations with Bill and arranged to visit him on my next research trip to the nearby New Forest area.

The more Bill spoke about him, the more I realised that Ernie Mason was indeed a most remarkable man.

Not long after I had met Bill, I was speaking to Jonathan Tapsell, author, of Hexagon Productions, and happened to mention him. He was keen to meet Bill, so I put them in touch with each other. Jonathan subsequently visited Bill on more than one occasion and published some of what he was told in two books.[1][2]

I have taken my own notes together with quotations from Jonathan's books to produce the fullest information we have and, I hope, in the process, to paint a vivid picture of Ernie Mason. I have not acknowledged all the quotations individually as there

---

[1] Jonathan Tapsell *Ameth: The Life and Times of Doreen Valiente* (Avalonia, 2014) pp. 40-41.
[2] Jonathan Tapsell *Psychic Jungle* (Lilith Mandrake Books, 2015) pp. 189-197.

was considerable overlap between what Bill told me and what he told Jonathan.

Ernie was born on 1st September 1885. He told Bill that he remembered being in his cradle, at about 18 months old, and that he "couldn't stand the silly nonsense" of the way people talked to him. Ernie told Bill that his mind was open from the month he was born.

17. Ernie Mason

Ernie was an engineer and chemist by profession and was quite a well-known person in the Portswood suburb of Southampton. While his father, George, was alive, he used to help him in the family lantern-slide business and, indeed, anything to do with optics, which led to his enthusiasm for astronomy and the construction of telescopes and observatories. Bill Wakefield remembers how Ernie helped him build a camera obscura in his attic.

Ernie had inherited his father's interest in astronomy and was a founder member of the Southampton Astronomical Society. Following war damage, Ernie had reconstructed the observatory that his father had built in the garden, with the help of members of the Astronomical Society.

The observatory contained an 18-inch reflecting telescope which Ernie had made himself - a remarkable achievement, involving working with mirror blanks, a grinding machine and plenty of carborundum to get a perfect finish; and a gearing mechanism to allow the telescope to keep pointing at the same part of the heavens as the Earth revolves. In fact, Ernie was awarded the honour of being made a Fellow of the Royal Astronomical Society.

His interest in optics was carried over into the activity by which he earned his living, which was, as already mentioned, lantern slide manufacture, a business he had inherited from his parents. The slides were two and a half inch square sheets of glass which were projected by a 'magic lantern' fuelled by paraffin. As well as manufacturing slides for others (including, it is rumoured, copies of the famous Cottingley fairy photographs for Sir Arthur Conan Doyle to illustrate his lectures), Ernie had a very large collection of slides on a variety of topics, the astronomical section of which was said to excel those of the British Astronomical Association. The slides were mainly in black-and-white, but some were hand-coloured, and others were mounted in a wooden framework and were capable of animation.

In fact, like his father before him, Ernie very much fitted the image of the 'eccentric inventor'. Before the war, for example, he was working on a method to produce good quality colour film. And he was, during the war, working at the request of the Government to see if he could provide the key to the release of 'sonic energy', which was thought to be a better way of obtaining explosives. This sounds fascinating and I wonder what it actually involved, but, in the absence of any more information on this, I merely note it.

Beechwood had been the family home since 1922 but by 1945 George and his wife, Rosetta, had died; their daughter, Rose, had married; and Susie had moved to Christchurch. So Ernie was living on his own in what had been a large family house. Bill, who used to be an airline steward, came to visit Ernie after every flight.

The house had a dark, dank cellar where Ernie kept his grinding machine. It was frequented by rats and spiders. He used to test his optics in the two bottom rooms. There was no central heating and Bill remembers the house being freezing, particularly the bedroom, and there were always mice running about.

There was a big room upstairs at Beechwood, which is where the Rosicrucians had their meetings. It had a carpet, 18ft square, in the traditional black-and-white pattern, which suggests it was first used by the Co-Masons, details of which I shall give in the next chapter. The room had what Bill described as "masses of books". There was also assorted "silver and wealth" from the Rosicrucians.

At one end of the room there was a large jade Buddha, 11 inches high by 9 inches wide. It was called 'Dafo', (a name we have already come across in other contexts) and was apparently used as a psychic battery filled with prayer power. Bill told me that Ernie had given it to Stroud Museum, but a friend enquired recently for me and they have no record of it. I remember visiting Stroud Museum in 1960 and at that time it was certainly rather disorganised though I imagine things will have changed for the better in the last 60 years.

The only heating seemed to be a gas ring under Ernie's chair. On one occasion, Bill had to rescue him when his trousers caught alight. Latterly, Ernie could not reach his feet and Bill had to bathe him. His feet were most unusual, being engrained with silver nitrate and carborundum. This was because he had worked for so long with silver salts and had been taught by his brother, Alf, to make his own silver nitrate. As a result his feet were stained bright silver. When he went to hospital for some minor treatment, the nurses marvelled at them and the medical people wanted to photograph them!

Unfortunately, Beechwood was demolished in connection with the construction of approach roads to Thomas Lewis Way in 1989.

But there was far more to Ernie Mason than the scientific side. There was another side, an esoteric side, and one that only revealed itself if the circumstances were right and if he thought the enquirer was genuinely interested. Bill had been attracted by the astronomy and had long talks with Ernie. One day, he asked him "Don't you ever think that there's something greater than us out there, something we might call 'God'?" Ernie replied "Only a fool would deny that!" That was the opening, and from there on, Ernie used to teach Bill and his brother Colin about a wide variety of esoteric matters.

Bill told me he considered Ernie to be a brilliant man but a hard task-master, who used to go through things very thoroughly. Ernie used to teach them mental exercises. Nothing was written down, but they weren't allowed to go on to the next exercise until they had mastered the current one.

The Rosicrucian influence was strong and Ernie always acknowledged the influence of George Alexander Sullivan as his teacher. We will discuss him and his Crotona Fellowship further in Chapter 6. Ernie had taken on the mantle of Sullivan's Crotona Fellowship with the demise of activities in Christchurch. He seems to have become custodian of the library and archives of the group (later donated to the University of Southampton), together with some of the Masonic regalia. Ernie had acquired a lot of other material from the Crotona Fellowship. Some of which, in turn, he gave to Bill - anvil; hammers; doves and birds of paradise (what these were I have no idea!); mallet; plumb bobs; set square etc. But the main thing that Ernie had acquired was the Rosicrucian teachings, which he was able to pass on to others in a remarkable way. Bill considered him to be a Magus and a born teacher, using parables and cartoons in the process.

In Bill's experience, many people used to come and consult Ernie because he had "a way of explaining things". These included lawyers, doctors, councillors and the commander of Portsmouth dockyard. Jonathan Tapsell recounts what Bill told him:

> *Old Ernie met people in a room above his workshop. Old Ernie was visited by many people from far and wide, business people, academics, well-to-do folk. People would come through the workshop and go to the room. ... When the meetings were convened I often heard chanting.*[3]

> *He was visited by lots of people, business people, rich folk, academics, and one I remember used to come in a chauffeur driven car. It was a Rolls Royce with a crest on the side. When these people came it was very hush-hush. Old Ernie just escorted them in through the workshop up into his chamber. We used to hear chanting sometimes coming from the room but we never asked questions. ... The Rolls Royce was dark, black I think. It came from the naval dockyards in Portsmouth and the guest was very important, he was "the" most important visitor I think. The car was always driven by a woman who also visited Old Ernie. It was very hush-hush.*[4]

Jonathan put forward the possibility that the important visitor was in fact Lord Mountbatten, who lived at Broadlands in nearby Romsey. He was known to have an interest in the occult and spiritualism. His driver was likely to have been Dolores North,

---

3   Tapsell 2015 p. 194.
4   Tapsell 2015 pp. 191-192.

otherwise known as Madeline Montalban, later a well-known writer on esoteric subjects.

Bill told me that one of Ernie's regular pupils was a Dr Harries, of Bristol University. Professor Ronald Hutton very kindly looked up the records and found no-one that matched that description, so Bill's memory, at least on that occasion, must have been faulty with regard to the name or the university or both!

Bill's use of the word 'pupil' suggests that Ernie gave what might be called "courses of instruction" as well as one-off consultations. Indeed, Bill and his friends, Harry Stubbs and Geoff Salt, undertook such a course.

Exactly what Ernie's teachings were it is difficult to determine. They certainly included the sort of Rosicrucianism taught by the Crotona Fellowship but also insights derived from Co-Masonry and Theosophy. Indeed, from what I have learned of Ernie, it would be very much his own teachings, somewhat eclectic. Also, he would never take a penny for any of his teachings.

Jonathan Tapsell says that Bill told him that Ernie was:

One of the most learned men he had ever encountered, holding a breadth and depth of knowledge few men could match. His interests included science, astronomy, biology, chemistry, medicine, chess, ciphers and codes, but in each he knew so much more than even the experts.

And Ernie certainly had psychic powers. All the family were mind-control people, but he was the most knowledgeable. Jonathan Tapsell wrote:

... Ernie possessed telepathic abilities; he also had the power to make objects materialise (apports) demonstrating this on one famous occasion in front of witnesses. Apparently a small group of people had been talking to Old Ernie in a room at his house when five stones appeared on a table. Old Ernie continued without commenting, but someone who picked the stones up found

them very warm to the touch. It was clear talking to Bill that Old Ernie had demonstrated similar feats to the Wakefield brothers.

Ernie could see auras. At the Rosicrucian Theatre in Christchurch, he and Sullivan used these abilities to decide how each of the performers could best be used.

He could also change the weather with his mind, something which Bill saw him do. And he had the knack of talking to those who had passed over, including his brother, Alf.

One of the most remarkable powers he possessed was the ability to walk on water, presumably a combination of levitation and mind control. Ernie used to tell the story of when he was out in a boat with a friend and they used to do things with their minds, one of them walking across the water. Sullivan saw this and said "Why do you have to show off?"

My interest in Ernie Mason was not just because of his great powers and knowledge but because he belonged to a family which I strongly suspected as being part of the group who, in 1939, initiated Gerald Gardner into witchcraft.

I was therefore particularly interested in what Bill Wakefield had to say on the subject. He told me:

> *Ernie was a witch as well as a Rosicrucian. The whole family were witches. They practised the White Order.*

There then follows a statement which Bill told both Jonathan and myself in identical wording, as if it was something that was very important to him and something which he had learned by heart. Ernie said to Bill:

> *I'm a white witch. Some people might say you were. You don't need to bother with any of this Crotona Fellowship, Co-Masonry or whatever. You've got beyond that.*

Bill told me that Ernie *had handed it on to a woman. Maybe tools, etc., maybe the knowledge, maybe the energy.*

He was more specific when talking to Jonathan. Bill told him that Ernie had passed the 'power' on to a woman in the 1950s:

> *It had to be a woman and she in turn would have to find a man to teach it all to ... It wasn't knowledge he passed on. It was power. An energy that had to [be] passed man to woman, woman to man.*

Jonathan believes this woman to have been Doreen Valiente. He may well be right. Having made contact with Dafo in late 1952, her powers of investigation would, I am convinced, eventually have led her to Ernie Mason.

Bill told Jonathan that Ernie once proclaimed: *I am the Guardian of the Ancient Oral Tradition of this Land.*

18. Ernie Mason in ritual robe outside Beechwood Hall 1953

One telling detail is that Ernie gave up the witch rituals in later life as he found them too strenuous. I can relate to this as I am getting to that stage in my own life!

Ernie finally felt unable to cope any longer at Beechwood and spent his last years at The Gables Nursing Home, 13 St. Mary's Road, Netley Abbey. He died on 26th February 1979 at the age of 93. He died of gastro-enteritis, apparently from food poisoning after eating a pork pie that he had kept in his pocket for some time.

───────────── ··•━◆━•·· ─────────────

The question that forms itself in our minds, however, is when did Ernie start calling himself a witch? Did it pre-date contacts made in Highcliffe and Christchurch? In other words, were the Masons a traditional witch family? Or did Ernie and his relatives merely add witchcraft to the long list of esoteric topics in which they were interested?

One clue is that Ernie called himself a "white witch" and said that he belonged to the White Order. We shall look at the implications of his use of that term in due course.

Whatever the truth, Ernie Mason was a remarkable man who influenced the lives of many who came into contact with him.

It is quite clear from what Bill Wakefield told Jonathan Tapsell and myself that Ernie Mason considered himself a witch. What we have to determine is whether he considered himself so before he met Edith and Rosamund; in other words, did the Mason family consider themselves witches before any of the others came along. I am inclined to believe that they did.

Writing in *Witchcraft Today* about what he called the witch cult, Gerald Gardner says of the witches he knew:

> *They know that their fathers and grandfathers belonged, and had spoken to them of meetings about the time of*

Waterloo, when it was then an old cult, thought to exist from all time.[5]

Grandfathers and grandmothers have told folk still living of meetings they attended about a hundred and thirty years ago, when the cult was thought to have existed from all time.[6]

Poor editing on the part of the publishers has resulted in two very similar statements on successive pages. Before examining their significance, however, it would be as well to look at the equivalent statement in an earlier version of the manuscript for the book, then to be entitled New Light on Witchcraft, one copy of which is now in the Toronto collection:

Grandfathers and ~~grandmothers~~ Great Grandmother have told folk still living of meetings they attended about a hundred and thirty years ago, when the cult was thought to have existed from all time.

And when referring to the ritual that the witches carried out in the New Forest in 1940 to put the idea into Hitler's mind that he could not cross the sea, Gardner writes: *The witches told me that their great-grandfathers had tried to project the same idea into Boney's mind.*

The clear implication behind Gardner's statement is that the witches concerned were of a hereditary tradition; in other words, ideas and techniques were passed down within the family.

It is also likely that those most concerned about a potential Napoleonic invasion would be those living close to the south coast of England.

Only one family, of all those we have and will look at in this book, meets these criteria, and that is the Mason family.

---

[5] Gardner (1954) p. 46.
[6] Gardner (1954) p. 47.

5
Dissent at Harmony Lodge

Harmony Lodge No. 25, Southampton, of International Co-Freemasonry was established in 1928, with meetings held at 32 Carlton Crescent in the city centre, the same building that was the location for the Southampton Lodge of the Theosophical Society from 1925.

In 1934, George Miles Mason had plans drawn up to erect a meeting hall within the grounds of Beechwood. This was a substantial building, 30 feet by 20 feet in area. It had full height windows on two sides and had its own kitchen and lavatory. It is described on the 1948 Ordnance Survey map as a Church Mission Hall. Whilst one does not lightly criticise the Ordnance Survey, particularly in matters concerning its home town of Southampton, it was actually nothing of the sort!

It was known as Beechwood Hall and seems to have been used for meetings of the various esoteric groups in which the family were interested. It was completed in late 1934 and was used initially by the newly-formed local lodge of the International Co-Freemasons.

Co-Masonry is a form of Freemasonry, the most distinguishing characteristic of which is that it is open to both men and women. It started in France in 1882, when Mlle Maria Deraismes was initiated into a Lodge under the jurisdiction of the Grande Loge Symbolique de France, in Pecq, a small town outside Paris. This was apparently not favoured by the Grande Loge and when, in 1883, after Dr Georges Martin, a high ranking member of the Grande Loge, had tried unsuccessfully to persuade them to form a lodge for women, he approached Mlle Deraismes and, as a result, a new lodge for both men and women was founded in

Paris. It was called the Grande Loge Symbolique Écossaise Mixte de France. In 1900, the Lodge established a Supreme Council to administer the Order and to take in the full 33 degrees of the Ancient and Accepted Scottish Rite.

Annie Besant (1847-1933) was a prominent socialist, theosophist and women's rights activist. She had become interested in Masonry, but had long felt that Masonry should be open to both men and women. On hearing about the French lodge, she applied to be initiated, and subsequently obtained permission to form the first lodge in Britain open to both men and women. On 26th September 1902, a Co-Masonic Lodge was consecrated in London by officers of the Supreme Council in Paris, and it was given the title Lodge Human Duty No. 6, of which she was the first ruler. The fact that Annie Besant was involved meant that there was a tendency towards an interest in esoteric and occult ideas amongst English members.

The new Temple for Harmony Lodge, No. 25, Southampton, Beechwood Hall, was consecrated on Sunday 13th January 1935. The Grand Commander, Mabel Besant-Scott, who was Annie Besant's daughter, and the Grand Secretary, D. Hodgson-Smith, were present at the ceremony of consecration:

> *The Consecrating Officer gave a warm welcome to the Brethren, pointing out that they had met to consecrate a new building, according to ancient usage; that all must help, for without solidarity there was no firm foundation to build to the Glory of T.G.A.O.T.U. ...* [The Great Architect of the Universe]

> *The delightful ceremony of receiving a Lewis* [the son or daughter of a Mason] *also took place, the infant daughter of Bros. Arthur and Edna Fudge being thus admitted into the Lodge.*

> *The effect upon all present on this wonderful day was the feeling of having touched real Free Masonry.*

Our illustration shows the four generations in the Lodge - something of a record.[1]

Perhaps the emphasis on solidarity was an inkling of problems which lay less than six months ahead and which threatened the very existence of Harmony Lodge.

There was undoubted disquiet within the British Federation of the Co-Masons and it all seemed to come to a head in the first two weeks of July 1935. It centred around the relationship between the British Federation and the Supreme Council in France. One major issue was that the Supreme Council had established 'fraternal relations' with the Grand Orient.

The Grand Orient de France was founded in 1733, but in 1877, in the strong anti-religious climate that was present following the defeat of Napoleon III, it abolished one of the basic Masonic principles, that of the necessity for Masons to profess a belief in a Supreme Being, and admitted atheists and free-thinkers into its lodges. It also went against another fundamental principle when it involved itself directly in politics. The rest of the Masonic world reacted by casting the Grand Orient out of the fold.

As well as being in 'fraternal relations' with this exiled body, the Supreme Council was also accused of "writing the Masonic secrets and having no belief in a Supreme Being". These criticisms came right from the top of the British Federation - from Mabel Besant-Scott. She is so important in our story that she has half a chapter to herself later in this book.

A petition had been circulated and Mabel wrote that there were those "who are truly torn between their loyalty to the Supreme Council and their loyalty to King and Country, which might become suspect, (they believe) on account of our relations with the Grand Orient ..." Some argued that the British Federation should break away from the Supreme Council.

---

[1] *The Bulletin - A Quarterly Journal of the British Federation International Co-Freemasonry* (April 1935).

Mabel continued:

> ... *members recognise with gratitude the great debt they owe to the Supreme Council for the great tolerance and liberty given to them since the beginning of our Masonic work. The Supreme Council is our masonic mother; but the children have arrived at the age of thirty-three years, the full masonic age, and should now leave their mother's house and build a house for themselves.*[2]

Several members of Harmony Lodge No. 25 in Southampton felt the same way. Ernie and Susie Mason and Gavin Harris circulated a letter drumming up support for secession from the jurisdiction of the Supreme Council. They continued:

> ... *the political situation in Europe is at present strained to breaking point, and trouble may be expected of so serious a nature that it behoves every British subject to free himself from any foreign entanglement - such as obedience to the Supreme Council of International Co-Freemasonry. ... the attitude of the present Consistory Council is such as would associate the Brethren with suspicion of political intrigue.*[3]

As a result, the Supreme Council for the British Federation suspended these three "from all Masonic rights and privileges" for what was described as "gross disloyalty".

In October 1935, there is a simple notice in *The Bulletin* which states: "The Charter of Lodge Harmony, Southampton, has been returned as the majority of the members of that Lodge resigned from the Order."

Apart from Mabel Besant-Scott herself, there did not appear to be any desire amongst the leaders of the British Federation to secede from the Supreme Council. So, in the end, virtually the whole of Harmony Lodge, certainly the most active members, including Ernie and Susie Mason and Edith Woodford-Grimes took the lead

---

[2] Letter from Mabel Besant-Scott to the M. P. Sov. Gr. Master 1 July 1935.
[3] Circular letter from Susie M. Mason, Ernest W. Mason and Gavin Harris 10 July 1935.

from Mabel Besant-Scott and resigned from the British Federation. Edith, for example, wrote:

> *I wish to tender my resignation from the Order of International Co-Freemasonry ... I feel I can no longer owe allegiance to the Supreme Council ... I am not insensible to the many privileges I have received from Co-Freemasonry and shall always acknowledge that debt.*[4]

Our story will shortly move some 20 miles to the south-west, to Somerford, a suburb of Christchurch, on the other side of the New Forest.

But first let us look more closely at the life of Mabel Besant-Scott, for it was because of her espousal of Rosicrucianism, and particularly of that branch of it that was being established in Somerford, that Edith and the Mason family followed her lead by similarly becoming involved.

---

[4]   Draft letter from Edith Woodford-Grimes to the Grand Secretary.

6
Bringing Pythagoras to Christchurch

As our story progresses, we will meet along the way certain individuals who play a part in it. Further on in the book, their role in our story will, I hope, become clearer.

One woman who indirectly features in and influenced our story was Mabel Besant-Scott. We met her in the previous chapter as head of the Co-Masons in Britain in 1935. Known to her friends as 'Mabs', Mabel Emily Besant Scott is important in our story of how Gerald Gardner first met the witches.

Born on 28th August 1870, she was the daughter of freethinker and theosophist, Annie Besant and her husband, Rev. Frank Besant, at Leckhampton, near Cheltenham, where he was the incumbent. Even at the time of her birth, her parents were not getting on personally, and the great ideological differences between them began to surface. Frank had apparently hit Annie when she ... *begged him not to force another child on her.*[1]

When she was only eight months old, Mabel, who was described as 'delicate', contracted whooping cough and then severe bronchitis. Anne Taylor says:

> *Annie retreated with her into a makeshift tent before the fire where steam from a succession of kettles vied with coal smoke for the good or ill of Mabel's lungs.*[2]

I remember my parents telling me that I almost died when I was a year old and my aunt told me that a similar remedy was given to me!

---

[1] Anne Taylor *Annie Besant: A Biography* (Oxford University Press, 1992) p. 35.
[2] ibid. p. 36.

Mabel's doctor gave her chloroform on a handkerchief to allay the severe coughing, apparently accepting the risks associated with that treatment because he believed she would not survive long. Probably as a consequence, she developed epilepsy, but she did survive, albeit as a frail child whose mother became over-protective towards her.

Annie left her husband in July 1873, taking Mabel and her elder brother, Digby, with her. Grounds for divorce at that time were limited to adultery, desertion and cruelty, whereas, as Anne Taylor says: *Heresy ... was really the issue between the Besants ...*[3] In any case, they both had religious objections to divorce, so a deed of separation was drawn up. This was permitted under the Custody of Infants Act, which had been passed earlier that year. It gave Annie the custody of Mabel, and Frank the custody of Digby, provided that each child spent a month every year with the other parent.

Frank Besant was never really happy with the arrangement, particularly when he obtained evidence that Mabel was not receiving religious instruction, which was in accordance with Annie's beliefs at the time. He petitioned the courts for the return of his daughter. The case hinged on whether Frank knew that Annie was not a Christian at the time he signed the original deed. The court decided that Annie should give Mabel up to her father and, as a consequence, Mabel spent the next ten years of her life at boarding school in Boston, Lincolnshire, living with her father in the holidays.

A campaign was fought against the decision. This included the production of photographs of her which bore the caption: *Mabel Emily Besant. Deprived of her mother, May 23, 1878. By Order of Sir George Jessel, Master of the Rolls, on account of that mother's heresy.*

---

3   ibid. p. 59.

19. Mabel Emily Besant as a young girl

However, by the age of 18, Mabel had started making clandestine visits to her mother, who by that time had become involved with Theosophy and was living at 19 Avenue Road, St John's Wood, and, as Anne Taylor says:

Before she came of age she went to live there permanently. The law was on Frank's side had he chosen to claim her. Instead he banished her as he had his son.[4]

---

4   ibid. p. 252.

In 1892, Mabel married Ernest Scott, a reporter on the *London Globe*. The same year they emigrated to Australia and their only child, Muriel, was born. Apparently at Mabel's insistence, they changed their surname to Besant-Scott. Mabel continued the interest in theosophy which she had acquired from her mother.

20. Mabel Besant Scott with her mother, Annie Besant, and her daughter Muriel

About 1896, however, Mabel became a Roman Catholic and was estranged from her husband. She returned to England in 1909. By this time, her mother was, and continued to be, heavily involved with Co-Masonry until her death in 1933. This attracted Mabel as well, and she was actively involved in founding various lodges. She rose steadily in Co-Masonry so that by the late 1920s she received the highest (i.e. 33) degree in Co-Masonry. She was appointed Deputy Supreme Council Representative in 1933, and in 1934, following the death of her mother, she was made Most Puissant Grand Commander of the British Federation, the top post.

Exactly how Mabel made contact with the Crotona Fellowship is uncertain, but I suspect that it was via her friendship with Catherine Chalk, who was a long-standing Co-Mason, and whose life we now look at.

The presence of the Rosicrucian Order Crotona Fellowship headquarters in Somerford, near Christchurch, on the edge of the New Forest, is due to one woman - Catherine Chalk. She is important in our story in ways which I shall recount in due course, but it may be worth now looking at her life and that of her husband, Thomas.

Catherine Chalk was born Catherine Emily Stringer on 20th June 1863 in Brighton, Sussex. Her parents were Katherine and the remarkably-named Stringer Stringer, who is described in the 1871 Census as a landowner. In that Census and in the previous one in 1861, the family were living at 22 Buckingham Place, Brighton, so that is probably where Catherine was born. However, previously Stringer Stringer had lived at Paynetts, a large house near the village of Goudhurst in Kent.

In 1896, Catherine married Thomas Chalk, who was born in Cambridge in 1861. His obituary in the *Christchurch Times* gives an account of his life, which I give below:

> *Born at Cambridge, Thomas Arthur Chalk was the only son of the late Rev. Thomas Chalk, formerly of Quainton, Bucks., and of Southbourne. We understand that his father was the first clergyman at Southbourne, where he was curate-in-charge, and he used often to preach at the Priory Church. When he first came to that district, fewer than a*

dozen houses existed there, and it was partly due to his boyhood's association with Southbourne that Major Chalk decided to spend his last years in Christchurch after a lifetime devoted to Empire building, in the course of which he had many exciting adventures.

Educated at Sherborne, Major Chalk, who was blessed with a wonderful constitution, was a very fine athlete in his youth, and gained numerous prizes at college.

With his death there passes another link in the chain of those great men of the Victorian era who did so much to build up our Empire. He first saw service in Egypt, where he was with the Camel Corps that went to the relief of General Gordon at Khartoum.

Later he was with the South African Mounted Police in the days of Dr. Jameson and Cecil Rhodes, and was one of the select few who became known as "Cecil Rhodes young men". He was appointed staff officer to Major Wilson, and on the very day that Major Chalk was taken to hospital suffering from dysentery, Major Wilson's force was ambushed and annihilated by the Matabeleland natives at Shanangi River in 1893. His illness therefore saved his life.

He was one of the expedition organised by Cecil Rhodes to take over the administration of Matabeleland with some 500 troops, and it took three months in bullock waggons to make the journey from the Cape to Fort Victoria.

Cecil Rhodes appointed Major Chalk administrator of a large area in the Matoppo Hills, and his administration proved highly successful. He learned the native language and studied their customs, and ultimately became a great power with the natives because he made a point, as far as possible, of administering the country according to the customs and traditions which passed for its laws. The native chiefs became devoted to him, and he could relate many strange tales of his dealings and "palavers" with them.

After some five years, illness compelled him to return to England, but he went to Africa again to the Boer War with Younghusband's Horse, remaining there until peace was declared.

He was on the Reserve of Officers, Royal West Kent Regiment, at the outbreak of the late war, but, to his regret, failed to pass the medical test for foreign service, his African experience having undermined his health with attacks of malaria and dysentery.

However, he performed much useful service at home, first as Remount Officer at Shorncliffe, later with the Home Defence Corps which had charge of the outer defences of South London, including Woolwich, and the last two years of the war he was stationed at Cork, in charge of the south coast defences of Ireland, retiring from the Army in September 1919.[5]

Perhaps the most interesting thing in the obituary is that it goes on to say:

... with [Catherine] *he performed a great work in* [Kent] *on behalf of the Co-Masonic Order, in which both of them took an active interest in Bournemouth and Southampton since taking up their residence here some six years ago.*

In 1911, prior to the First World War, the Chalks were living at The Hutch, Seabrook, Hythe, Kent. Catherine is described as a Teacher of Music and Thomas as a Teacher of Singing. They had probably lived there since 1905, as there is a newspaper report of a Grand Concert in nearby Folkestone where Catherine performed as pianist and Thomas as a baritone. The report stated that they *have recently taken up residence in the neighbourhood of Folkestone.[6]* They may well have been working at the nearby Seabrook Lodge School, opened in 1900.

---

5   *Christchurch Times* 11 December 1931.
6   *Folkestone, Hythe, Sandgate and Cheriton Herald* 30 September 1905.

We do not know where they were living the previous year but there is a newspaper report of a concert at Minehead which makes it clear that Catherine was also a composer. It refers to:

> *Captain Chalk's second contribution was the song "There is ever a Song somewhere", another graceful composition by Mrs. Chalk, to which he did full justice, and again the audience recognised the merit of the song and the way in which it was rendered by according an encore.*[7]

By 1925, the Chalks had moved to Somerford, a suburb of Christchurch, Hampshire.

One of the movements that Catherine Chalk was interested in was Rosicrucianism. It did not reside within any one organisation. Rather it was a movement which formed part of the Western esoteric tradition. It had its roots in Gnosticism, Kabbalism and several other strands. It really started with certain documents which were published in Germany at the beginning of the 17th Century. The anonymous Fama Fraternitatis explained how the Order of the Rosy Cross was founded by a mysterious figure known as Christian Rosenkreutz, who was born in the 14th or 15th Century. The movement spread throughout Europe, including England, and many have claimed that Francis Bacon (1561-1626) was a member. There is a belief, popular particularly amongst Rosicrucians, that Bacon was the author of the Shakespeare plays. Christopher McIntosh, however, points out that Bacon was actually not very sympathetic to the occult and that his writing style was very different from that of Shakespeare.[8] There were probable links with Freemasonry from the earliest days, and certainly by the mid-18th Century there were specific Rosicrucian Masonic degrees. In 1865, the Societas Rosicruciana in Anglia (S.R.I.A. or Soc. Ros.) was founded, reputedly based on old documents found in Freemasons' Hall. Membership was limited to Master Masons, one of whom claimed initiation from German Rosicrucian adepts.

---

[7] *West Somerset Free Press* 9 April 1904.

[8] Christopher McIntosh *The Rosicrucians - The History, Mythology and Rituals of an Esoteric Order* (Aquarian, 1980; revised edition Weiser, 1997) p. 100.

Catherine Chalk was particularly interested in an organisation known as the Rosicrucian Order Crotona Fellowship, which was formed in Liverpool in 1920 by one George Alexander Sullivan (1890-1942). It is possible that this may have had some link with the Order of the Temple of the Rose Cross, which was founded in 1912 by Annie Besant in connection with the Theosophical Society. It is understood, however, that this had collapsed in 1918.

Many slim publications, mostly written by Sullivan, who made his living as a journalist, appeared, printed on his own press. From Liverpool, Sullivan started a correspondence course. The main influences seem to have been Rosicrucian tradition, Theosophical ideas and Masonic practices, together with Sullivan's personal contribution, often by means of inspired or guided writings which he issued under the name of Aureolis. This is the middle name of Paracelsus (though sometimes spelt 'Aureolus'), a Renaissance medic and occultist, who was thought, certainly by Sullivan, to have been a Rosicrucian.

In July 1935, the very month when the dissent at Harmony Lodge reached its climax, a new publication, entitled *The Uplifting Veil* was produced by the Crotona Fellowship. It was a slightly more elaborate publication than the simple pamphlets previously produced by Sullivan, as if there were a new enthusiasm. It included a major contribution by Catherine Chalk, an article entitled 'Kabalistic Keys to Aryan Myths' which looks at parallels between the Tree of Life and the myths underlying the Wagnerian dramas. She concludes:

> *Secret Wisdom teaching may present some less known aspects of Aryan Myths. They are strung upon an unbroken thread, the thread of Ariadne, and woven into the heart of life in all ages for the guidance of man, pointing out a pathway, lit by the gleams of spiritual rays, which shine more or less clearly, as our understanding is able and ready to perceive them.*[9]

---

[9] C E Chalk 'Kabalistic Keys to Aryan Myths' *The Uplifting Veil* Vol 1 No 1 July 1935) pp. 11-13.

Catherine gave talks, on Shakespeare's London at the Ashrama Hall[10] and on Wagner's play, *Parsifal*.[11] She also spoke on 'The Stage in the Time of Shakespeare' to the Highcliffe Literary and Debating Society. In the report in the *Christchurch Times* she is described as the well-known local authority on the days of the Early English Theatre.[12]

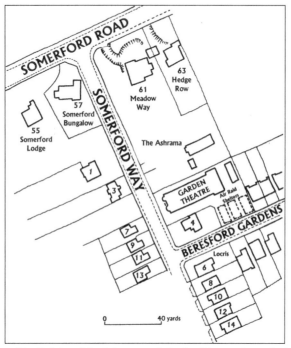

21. The Vicinity of the Ashrama and Garden Theatre, Somerford
(based on the 1939 Ordnance Survey map)

In 1935 came the move of the Crotona Fellowship headquarters to Somerford. Catherine Chalk, following the death of her husband in 1931, offered her house, Meadow Way, off Somerford Road, and substantial garden, to the Fellowship and moved into a smaller house next door. A wooden building, known as the Ashrama Hall, was erected in the garden the following year, and the Fellowship

---

[10] *Christchurch Times* 5 March 1938.
[11] *Christchurch Times* 9 April 1938.
[12] *Christchurch Times* 26 November 1938.

started having its meetings there. These involved study, religious ritual and dramatics.

The philosophy of the Crotona Fellowship, which followed established Rosicrucian teachings, can perhaps be summarised as being the belief that we are not just a physical body; that there is a part of us that survives physical death and is reborn; that our many lifetimes are periods of learning by experience; and that we are all potentially capable of great things, having esoteric faculties we can use and develop to help ourselves and others to make spiritual progress.

I wrote about the Crotona Fellowship's beliefs and practices in more detail in my book, *Wiccan Roots*.[13] Gerald Gardner, Edith Woodford-Grimes, Susie, Ernie and Rosetta Mason, amongst others, were all members of the Crotona Fellowship and, whether they admitted it or not, were all influenced by its philosophy.

At what stage after the troubles at Harmony Lodge in 1935, Edith and the Masons decided to attend meetings of the Crotona Fellowship I do not know, but I imagine that it would be fairly quickly.

Bracelin writes that they "[followed] Mabs to her settlement".[14] This was not, at any rate at first, a physical move but a philosophical one.

We can imagine concern for the future of Co-Masonry building up throughout the first half of 1935 amongst the members of Harmony Lodge, and there was undoubtedly an interchange of ideas and suggestions between them and Mabel Besant-Scott during that crucial six month period. Mabel had undoubtedly been kept informed by Catherine Chalk among, I am sure, others of the developments in Somerford and of the Crotona Fellowship's decision to move its headquarters from Liverpool.

---

13 op. cit.
14 Bracelin p. 166.

22. EdithWoodford Grimes in academic dress as she gained her Rosicrucian degree

But we now look at the lives of several other individuals who also played an important part in our story.

7
Rose of the World

Dafo and the Mason family had started attending meetings of the Crotona Fellowship in Christchurch by mid 1935. Bracelin writes of Gerald: He found that his friends, after following Mabs to her settlement, had discovered an old Coven, and remained here because of that.[1]

But can we take it further and identify some members of a possible New Forest coven?

In this chapter, we will explore the life and work of a fascinating character who was, I believe, central to the whole enterprise.

I was taught when young never to write in books. I have reluctantly overcome this habit sufficiently to "personalise" my published books when a potential reader requests it, but to make notes in the margins was definitely not on.

Luckily for our researches, author and witch, Doreen Valiente was not one to have such inhibitions.

I had been invited down to Sussex to stay with John and Julie Belham-Payne, who had inherited Doreen's collection of artefacts as well as her archive of papers and extensive library.

It was while looking through that library that I came upon Doreen's copy of the biography *Gerald Gardner Witch*.

It is a fascinating story of Gerald Gardner's life: his childhood, his working life out east and his retirement to England in 1936. As al-

---

[1] Bracelin p. 166.

ready mentioned, what interested me when I first read it was Chapter 13 entitled 'Into the Witch Cult'. I was glancing through this very familiar chapter when, on page 166, I noticed a marginal annotation in Doreen's handwriting. The author is writing about the old coven which Gardner's friends claimed to have discovered. Directly quoting Gardner, he wrote a passage which read: *I found that Old Dorothy and some like her, plus a number of New Forest people, had kept the light shining.* We shall look at the life of 'Old Dorothy' in a future chapter, but what struck me was that, after the phrase 'New Forest people', Doreen had put an asterisk and written in the margin two words: Mother Sabine.

When I noticed this, I suddenly realised that we appeared to have the name of another member of the coven, Mother Sabine. It was an exciting moment for me!

But how could I take this further? The first thing I asked myself was whether 'Sabine' was a personal name or a surname, for it can, of course, be either. Using the same principle as looking for lost keys under a streetlight, I opted for a surname, and asked my friend, Ian Stevenson, the local historian in Highcliffe, to look up Sabine in his collection of local street directories. There were only two entries in the whole of the Bournemouth/Christchurch area, one of which was in Avenue Road, Highcliffe, the very street where Edith Woodford-Grimes was living. I decided to pursue this one! Living at 'Whinchat' in Avenue Road were Thomas George Alford Broadfield Sabine and his wife, Rosamund Isabella Charlotte Sabine. They married in 1911 and their marriage certificate showed that Rosamund's maiden name was Carnsew.

Rosamund was born at Somers Place, Billingshurst, Sussex on 5th February 1865. Her father was Henry Carnsew (26 April 1826 – 22 September 1891), a solicitor, and her mother was Henrietta Maria Carnsew, formerly Donnithorne (18 August 1837 to 4 September 1865). Both came from long-established Cornish families. The names 'Isabella Charlotte' seem to have been in memory of

Rosamund's aunt, Isabella Charlotte Donnithorne, who died in 1855 aged twenty.

In my book, *Gerald Gardner and the Cauldron of Inspiration*[2], I made a serious mistake in that I did not spot the entry for Rosamund in the Register of Births microfiches when I was looking for her in Hull Central Library. I don't know how I missed her, but I did. These things happen, but I now have the opportunity, over 15 years later, to give the correct details and the profusion of facts which spring from them.

On 17th March 1864, Henry Carnsew married Henrietta Maria Donnithorne at Trinity Church, Twickenham, Middlesex. Under "Rank or Profession", both Henry and their fathers are indicated as "Esquire", in other words, of private means.

The Carnsews lived in Lostwithiel in Cornwall in the mid 18th Century. By the early 19th Century, and certainly by the time Henry was born, in 1826, the family was well established in the small village of Poughill, on the north coast of Cornwall.

How Henry met his wife I do not know. Whilst the Carnsews and Donnithornes were both prominent Cornish families, St Agnes and Poughill are some 45 miles apart with no easy links between them, so I think it is more likely that they met when both of them were living in the London area.

We do not know why Henry and his wife chose Rosamund as a name. Perhaps because Matthew Rosamund had been the recipient of the Victoria Cross in 1857 and had received some publicity at the time.

I will discuss Rosamund's name in greater detail than would normally be justified, because I have found, as will be revealed later in this book, that her names seemed to lead on organically to some of her interests and activities. As I will show later, Rosamund

2   Philip Heselton *Gerald Gardner and the Cauldron of Inspiration* (Capall Bann, 2003) p. 65.

gained inspiration for her esoteric studies from both her personal name and her surname.

The name Rosamund originates in the Old Germanic name of Rosamunda, meaning horse ('hros') protection ('mund'). It is, however, frequently associated with the Latin 'rosa mundi' meaning 'rose of the world'. An alternative Latin phrase, 'rosa munda' means 'pure rose'.

There was a Lombard queen named Rosamund, living in a time of war. With her lover, Helmichis, she plotted the murder of her husband, Alboin. She was later murdered by her lover. It was a classic tragedy, told many times in Italy and, in 1899, Algernon Charles Swinburne's Rosamund, Queen of the Lombards was published, a work with which, I am sure, our Rosamund would have been familiar.

Rosamund Clifford was a mistress of Henry II (1133-1189), said to be the love of his life. The king is supposed to have hidden her in a maze constructed in his park at Woodstock in Oxfordshire, which became known as Rosamund's Bower. She retired to God-stow Abbey, near Oxford.

By 1858, Henry Carnsew was living at 3 Berkeley Square, London, a prestigious address. By 1861, at the age of 35, he had progressed in his chosen profession of solicitor and became a Parliamentary Agent, a solicitor who was licensed by Parliament to draft private bills. This, and other work, obviously proved lucrative, for by 1861 he was living with his sister, Margaret, at 5 Chapel Street, St George Hanover Square.

Henry began to acquire land and buildings in the Billingshurst area of Sussex in 1860 while he was living in London. Why he should have chosen this particular village I do not know, but the same year he moved to Gratwicke House, south of East Street in the village.

Around this time, he had acquired Somers Place (also frequently known as "Summers Place"), a property which probably dates back to the 14th century, a mile or so north of Billingshurst, but leased it out for a while before moving there to live in 1863.[3]

The present house dates substantially from 1880, being built by a subsequent owner, Robert Goff. The house as it was known by Henry was much more modest. Tite notes the following:

> *It was during Henry Carnsew's time that Summers Place began to take on some of its present shape, even though the reconstruction of the main house was not to follow until 1880. A detailed survey was made in 1869 for a set of sale particulars, and this map shows the original farm buildings demolished and new ones erected to the north-east. A lodge had also been built, and the general structure of the gardens as we now see them, with the walk through the woods back to Stane Street, were established by Mr. Carnsew.[4]*

Henry seems to have been quite a benefactor to the village. In 1865 he gave land and money for the construction of a school:

> *There is a National school for boys and girls, supported by voluntary contributions: and a handsome new school-room has lately been erected: it is a simple Gothic building capable of accommodating about 150 children, with play grounds and master's residence attached: the building, which is of red brick, with stone dressings, has been built at the sole cost of Mr Carnsew (who also gave the site).[5]*

Henry also paid for the restoration of the parish church carried out in 1866, including two new stained glass east windows in the chancel and chapel. He dedicated the east window of the north aisle to the memory of Rosamund's mother, Henrietta Maria, who died on 4th September 1865 when Rosamund was less than

3   Graham Tite *Six Pence and a Rose: Summers Place and Sussex History* (Sotheby's, 1986)
4   ibid. p. 7.
5   Kelly's Directory 1897.

seven months old, apparently from complications arising from her birth.

I suspect that Henry somewhat lost interest in the village after his wife died. The house, even in its unextended state, was much too big for him and by 1869 the property was put up for sale.

I also suspect that Henry felt incapable of looking after Rosamund, particularly as he was frequently away on business, and so he arranged that she be looked after by her maternal grandfather, Edward Harris Donnithorne, and his wife, Georgina Donnithorne, who lived at Colne Lodge, Hanworth Road, Twickenham, Middlesex.

The Donnithornes were an old well-established Cornish family, originating in the village of St. Agnes, close to the wild Atlantic coast, near the town of Perranporth. There is a rather doubtful origin for the name: a shipwrecked Spaniard by the name of Don Thoan.[6]

They seemed to be a fairly well-to-do family for Nicholas Donnithorne (1669-1737), a tin blower, i.e. a tin smelter, became High Sheriff of Cornwall. The family had built a white painted tower, variously known as St Ann's Summer House; the Pleasure House; or Unwin and Donnithorne's Castle, on St Agnes Beacon, a coastal hilltop where flares could be lit in the event of invasion.

Clive Benney wrote a whole book about Rosemundy House, which was built on land, also called Rosemundy, which had been owned by the Donnithornes. I think that the memory of this interestingly named plot of land may have been in Rosamund's parents' minds when deciding on her name. What the origin of the name 'Rosemundy' may have been is open to conjecture. To quote Clive Benney:

> *The Donnithornes were a Cornish family that ran Polberro Mine, one of the richest mines in Cornwall, producing*

---

6   Burke's Landed Gentry 1862.

profits of £100 a day and employing 250 workers. Nicholas Donnithorne was High Sheriff of Cornwall in 1731 and lived at Trevallas Manor near St Agnes. On his death all his assets were inherited by his eldest son Joseph. In 1762 Joseph died, and all land and property were then inherited by Joseph's younger brother, the Revd Isaac Donnithorne (1709-1782), who had been ordained an Anglican priest in 1735.[7]

Rosamund's great-grandfather, James Donnithorne (1773-1852), was an employee of the East India Company, becoming a Judge and Master of the Mint for the Bengal Civil Service, retiring in 1838 to live in Australia.

James' son, Edward Harris Donnithorne (1810-1885), Rosamund's grandfather, was born in India and in 1834 he married Elizabeth Jane Moore in Topsham, Devon. He joined the 16th Lancers and was stationed in India.

Edward and Elizabeth had five children, Edward George Moore Donnithorne (1842-1906); Isabella Charlotte Donnithorne (1836-1855); Henrietta Maria Donnithorne (1837-1865), Rosamund's mother; Mary Penelope Donnithorne (1839 - 1918) and Arthur Bampton Donnithorne (1844-1885).

The Donnithornes were an interesting family, perhaps the most interesting being Rosamund's great aunt, Eliza Emily Donnithorne (1821-1886). In 1846, she moved to Australia to be with her father. The story goes that she soon got engaged to an aspiring politician named Stuart Donaldson. They were due to be married in 1848, but she was jilted by him and she lived in seclusion for the rest of her life.[8]

Evelyn Juers has carried out a considerable amount of research into Eliza's story. She writes, in her book, *The Recluse*:

---

[7] Clive Benney *The Secrets of Rosemundy House* (Wheal Hawke Publications, 2014) p. 7.

[8] Evelyn Juers *The Recluse* (Giramondo Publishing, 2012).

Was she jilted? No one really knows what happened. Possibly her father - a man not to be trifled with - tried to arrange matches for her with men like Donaldson, and she rejected them. In an era when women of her class were expected to marry suitably, it's to her credit that she did not become a pawn in colonial dynastics.

It's said she met someone she loved, her father objected to their marriage but then gave in, and on the wedding day the groom did not turn up. From that moment on, in case he was delayed, Eliza is supposed to have suffered an extreme form of lovesickness, worn her wedding dress for the rest of her life and over four decades kept the wedding feast laid out.[9]

Juers points out, however, that :

Not only has no evidence of the intended wedding been found, there's also significant uncertainty about the date. ... My hunch is, that jilted or not jilted, Eliza became a recluse and this fact was strange enough for the rest of the story in all its florid detail to grow around her.[10]

Writers, researchers and journalists wrote extensively about Eliza, but Juers concludes:

I suspect these writers simply chased a good story, emptied Eliza Donnithorne's life of its humdrum and filled it with the fanciful transcriptions of an urban myth.[11]

She quotes the very ancient sexton of St. Stephen's, who said:

It's all bunkum ... there wasn't any wedding arranged for any missing bridegroom ... Because Miss Donnithorne became a recluse people decided there had to be a reason and provided a romantic one.[12]

---

[9] ibid. p 65.
[10] ibid. pp 65-66.
[11] ibid. p 72.
[12] ibid. p 78.

It is thought by some that she was the individual upon whom Charles Dickens based the character of Miss Havisham in his novel *Great Expectations*.[13] Certainly Dickens knew the Donnithornes, visiting them several times, during which there was ample opportunity to learn of Eliza's story. It is a tale which has continuing appeal, and in 1974, the composer Peter Maxwell Davies wrote the song cycle Miss Donnithorne's Maggott which tells Eliza's story in musical form.[14]

———————————·•──■◆■──•·———————————

Now swallowed up by the relentless suburbanisation of London, Twickenham is a town on its south-western approaches, made world famous to many by its Rugby Football ground.

In the mid-19th Century, which is where we are currently focused, it was merely a village in the county of Middlesex. But its proximity to London and road improvements which had taken place in the 18th Century saw the erection of large 'villas' in their own substantial grounds on the edge of the village.

One of these was Colne Lodge. It occupied a plot of land to the west of the village, in the area known as Twickenham Common, stretching from Hanworth Road (now Staines Road) north to the banks of the River Crane.

Colne Lodge was a Palladian-style villa, built about 1765 to designs by Isaac Ware. It was a substantial three-storey house, set back from the road, having a large lawn and mature trees between it and the highway. In later years it had a tennis lawn to the rear of the house, with a paddock beyond stretching down to the river, with what may have been a fishing lake at the bottom. There was also a tower at the far end of the garden looking out across the River Crane, which might actually have been built on top of an ice house.

---

[13] First published 1861.
[14] Peter Maxwell Davies *Miss Donnithorne's Maggot and other stories* DVD (Artists Recording Company, 2013).

23. Colne Lodge in 1890

The house was demolished in the early 20th Century, and a new road, Meadway, was built along the length of the garden together with smaller houses. However, at the far end of the garden, closest to the river, the land has remained undeveloped. When visiting the site recently I was pleased to see that it had been adopted as a community orchard, and I met some of those involved in this enterprise. Now known as Meadway Orchard, it has been designated as a Site Of Nature Importance. I feel that Rosamund would have been pleased to see this.

24. Colne Lodge (John Spyers 1786)

Paul Whitehead (1710-1774), poet and satirist, was an early resident, from 1767 until his death seven years later. He wrote of the view out from the rear of Colne Lodge, possibly from the garden tower, as follows:

Here Campbell's varied shades with wonder see
Like Heav'n's own Eden, stor'd with every tree;
Each plant with plant in verdant glory vies;
High tow'ring pines, like Titans scale the skies;
And Lebanon's rich groves on Hounslow's desert rise.

(Epistle to Dr Thompson)[15]

As well as being a poet and satirist, Whitehead was secretary and steward to the Hell-Fire Club. Evelyn Juers describes this as:

... a secret society led by Sir Francis Dashwood, later known as Baron Le Despencer, which was rumoured to have met in caves deep under West Wycombe Hill, where members indulged in esoteric underground mischief, and at nearby Medmenham Abbey, where the gardens and interior design are said to have been erotically themed. Thompson wrote, Among other amusements, they had sometimes a mock celebration of the more ridiculous rites of the foreign Religious Order of the Church of Rome. Other amusements involved women, fancy dress, rituals, and excessive food and alcohol. Horace Walpole called them hermits, to me they seem extremely sociable. The club motto was the Rabelaisian Fais ce que tu voudrais, inscribed over the doorway of the abbey.[16]

The Club seems to have been an excuse for debauchery amongst the higher echelons of society with the trappings of esoteric beliefs and practices.

---

[15] Edward Thompson (ed.) *The Poems And Miscellaneous Compositions Of Paul Whitehead With Explanatory Notes Of His Writings, And His Life* (S. Price, W. Watson, et al, 1777).

[16] Juers pp. 40-41.

25. Paul Whitehead

Whitehead died on 30th December 1774. Evelyn Juers writes:

> *It's said that Whitehead knew too many secrets of too many powerful people, and a few days before his death, possibly suicide, he burnt all his papers in a great bonfire in the garden at Colne Lodge.*[17]

Whitehead's biographer, Thompson, states that he spent three days destroying his papers, but adds that he gleaned many from the fatal conflagration. It is perhaps worth remembering this when considering Rosamund's time spent at Colne Lodge. One might speculate that a young and enthusiastic Rosamund might have tracked down some of those papers, perhaps in the attic or the tower at the bottom of the garden, and that reading them started her on her esoteric studies. More likely, she may have learned about Whitehead from family members or neighbours and subsequently read further about him and the Hell Fire Club.

---

17 ibid. p. 41.

In addition, David Thomas thinks that:

It would be no surprise to find a family of this substance had Masonic connections, nor would it be unreasonable to suggest a knowledge of Indian philosophy or yogaic practices. Perhaps spending her formative years in this household sparked Rosamund's interest in mysticism.[18]

Anyway, after a succession of owners in the intervening 67 years from Whitehead's demise, Colne Lodge was purchased by the Donnithorne family in 1841.

———————————— •—◆—• ————————————

Following Rosamund's birth, Henry seems to have had financial difficulties, and by May 1870, bankruptcy proceedings were being made against him. A notice appeared in *The London Gazette*[19] notifying him that a petition was being served against him and that, if he did not appear in Court on 15th June 1870, the Court might adjudge him bankrupt in his absence.

The implication is that Henry could not be found, and it is likely that he was by then living in Belgium. As a solicitor, he was probably used to making money fairly readily, but also, it would seem, losing it equally readily. The threat of bankruptcy in 1870 seems to have been the cause of his move to Belgium.

Exactly what Henry was doing following the death of Henrietta Maria we do not know. However, in the Parish Church of Whitegate, Corkbegg, Midleton, Cork, Ireland, he married Hilda Mary Agnes Worsley on 25th July 1867, who at the time was living with her father at Roche Mount, County Cork.

Hilda was born on 29th November 1843 at Imberholme, East Grinstead, Sussex. Her mother was Juliana Agnes Mary Wright, born in 1820 in Marylebone, London, and her father was Frederick Cayley Worsley, born 6th February 1803 in Stonegrave,

---

[18] David Thomas letter to the author 5 May 2006.
[19] *The London Gazette* 17 May 1870.

Yorkshire. His brother was Sir William Worsley, baronet, of nearby Hovingham Hall. He seems also to have been connected to the Cayley baronets of Brompton, one of whom was the aviation pioneer, Sir George Cayley (1773-1857).

By 1870 Henry and Hilda were living in Belgium. Their main address at the end of 1879 was Brussels, from which he sometimes made visits to England. At the same time he was *in some measure dependant upon my pen.*[20]

It seems as if Henry needed to earn money in ways other than from the law. He had obviously learned French well enough during his time in Belgium to be capable of finding work as a translator. In one incident in 1879, Henry had translated a story for the popular *Temple Bar*, described as 'A London magazine for town and country readers'. The piece concerned was entitled 'The Sealed Letter' and it appeared in the November 1879 issue (pp 372-390). It had no indicator of author or translator. In fact, the author was the French poet, Alfred de Vigny (1797-1863).

Henry was quickly apprised of the situation, however, for on 2 December 1879 he wrote to the publisher:

> *The paper may be by Alfred de Vigny although I certainly never met with it in his works. I read it in a book called Contes Populaires, published in 1838. ... I need scarcely say that I had not the slightest intention of misleading you in any way & had I received any notice of the acceptance of the paper, or had the proof been sent to me, for correction I should probably have [illegible word] it "From Contes Populaires" ...*[21]

The translation is very good and readable. In fact, in my opinion, it was rather better than some more recent translations, which suggests that Henry had become quite adept at it and may well have been doing it on a regular basis.

---

[20] Bentley Corresp., University of Illinois.

[21] Bentley Corresp. University of Illinois, reel 24. Additions and Corrections to The Wellesley Index August 2006 Edition Eileen M Curran website.

In 1870, Hilda gave birth in Brussels to a daughter, Hilda Clara Frances Carnsew, a half-sister to Rosamund.

Perhaps it was this start of a new family for Henry that made him think that he was then in a position to look after Rosamund. He approached the Donnithornes on this issue, but they obviously rejected this idea because the next thing we hear is that the following year, in May 1871, Henry applied to the courts for permission to take Rosamund back into his care:

In the Court of Chancery, in "Re Carnsew - Carnsew v. Carnsew," a petition has been presented by Henry Carnsew, praying that his daughter, who is six years of age and a ward of Court, may be delivered over to his care and guidance as her natural guardian by Mr. Donnithorne, her maternal grandfather, with whom she has for some time past resided. The application was strenuously opposed by Mr. Donnithorne. It appears that Mr. Carnsew, who is a solicitor, some time ago became involved in financial difficulties which caused him to leave England for the Continent, where he now resides. It was objected by Mr. Donnithorne, who has maintained and educated the child since her father left the country, that it was contrary to the practice to allow a ward to be taken permanently abroad, and that Mr. Carnsew was not able to maintain and educate the child as well as she was being educated at present. It should be stated that the mother of the child is dead, and that Mr. Carnsew has married again.

The Master of the Rolls said that it was a painful case, which ought to have been arranged out of court. In deciding on applications as to the custody of wards the Court looked solely to the benefit of the ward, as a ground for controlling the legal right of the father. That was the principle established in "Lyons v. Blenkin" (Jac. 245), where a father applied that his children might be delivered up to him by their aunt, who was guardian of their fortunes, and with whom he had permitted them to reside for a long time, and Lord Eldon directed a reference to the Master to inquire by whom, and at what expense, the children had been educated, and whether the father was of sufficient ability to educate them in as beneficial a manner; and, if not, to approve a scheme for their education during their minorities. Besides this, it was the practice not to allow wards to be removed out of the jurisdiction unless for their health, and then with security for their returning to this country; but in the present instance there was no evidence that the health of the infant required her removal abroad, and no prospect of her return, as her father could not return.

After hearing the evidence as to Mr. Carnsew's circumstances he could not but doubt the possibility of Mr. Carnsew and his present wife maintaining the child as well as Mr. Donnithorne could and did maintain her. Upon the whole, therefore, he thought it would be most for the benefit of the child to leave her with Mr. Donnithorne; and he should make an order to that effect on Mr. Donnithorne undertaking to maintain the child in the same manner as he had hitherto done, Mr. Carnsew to have liberty to apply in Chambers respecting access to the child.[22]

Henry seemed to be the sort of person who liked to live in grand residences, perhaps too elaborate for his needs, and, more probably, his means. Certainly it seems as if the legal difficulties which prevented Henry Carnsew's return from Belgium whilst the bankruptcy court case was going on and the difficulties over country of residence seemed to have been resolved by 1881, as he was back in England.

In that year, he is living at 16th century Merdon Manor, Hursley, near Winchester, Hampshire, with his second wife, Hilda Mary Agnes, and their 10-year old daughter, Hilda Clara Frances Carnsew, together with three servants.

---

[22] See e.g. *The Solicitors' Journal and Reporter* Vol 15 p 492; *West Somerset Free Press* 6 May 1871.

It is clear from Rosamund's future activities and interests that she was well educated. Whether her grandparents employed a governess or sent her to school I do not know. There was a long-standing endowment under the wills of John and Frances West in 1720 to send boys and girls living in Twickenham to Christ's Hospital School, a boarding school in London. However, being relatively close to London, Rosamund might well have attended a day-school in Twickenham or neighbouring Richmond. I have not yet found where this might have been.

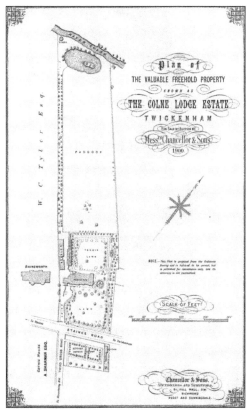

26. Colne Lodge: Plan accompanying sale document 1900

Rosamund was probably still living at Colne Lodge when her grandfather, Edward Donnithorne, died in 1885. It seems likely that her uncle, Arthur Bampton Donnithorne (1844-1885) then briefly looked after her until his own death. I suspect that the following year, when she was 21 and thus of "full age", she took matters into her own hands and started living with her father again. This is particularly likely as Henry's second wife, Hilda, had died in 1884. Rosamund probably felt that her father needed her.

27. Edward Harris Donnithorne, Rosamund's grandfather

Rosamund and her half-sister, Hilda, seemed to grow close to each other and did many things together. In January 1891, they attended a house party at Burton House, near Sutton in west Sussex.[23] This was somewhere with which Rosamund was to be closely associated for the next twenty years. Whether they were living in the area at that time I do not know, but they were obviously friendly with the Wright-Biddulph family who owned the House and Park and who were well-known Roman Catholics.

Just three months later, however, we find that Rosamund and Hilda are living with their father and his brother-in-law, John, at

---

[23] *Sussex Agricultural Express* 17 January 1891.

Treago Castle, in the parish of St. Weonards, Herefordshire. Treago Castle is a fortified manor house dating from about 1500. It was built round a quadrangle with defensive corner towers, although never subject to attack. It has long been associated with the Mynors family. It is situated in extensive parkland with mature trees.

How long they had been living there I do not know, but it seems to be typical of Henry to live in quite opulent surroundings in different parts of the country, a lifestyle which, certainly for a while, seems to have been emulated by his daughters. This suggests that he had the means to do this, but how this is compatible with his bankruptcy in 1870 I am not sure. Perhaps he was able subsequently to build up his fortune again.

Henry died on 22nd September 1891 but, perhaps strangely for a professional solicitor, he died intestate, in other words without making a will. Or perhaps he was being clever in not making one, for financially beneficial reasons that legal brains more perceptive than my own might be able to determine. However, Letters of Administration were granted to Rosamund and Hilda on 16th November 1891, by which time they were living at The Deanery, Exeter.

The Deanery is situated opposite the west front of Exeter Cathedral. It dates from the 15th Century but has been much altered. I imagine this would have been temporary lodgings for Rosamund and Hilda following their father's death before they could move into more permanent accommodation. The Donnithornes certainly had family connections in the Exeter area, including clergy, so I suspect these lodgings were offered to them after they had to move out of Treago following their father's death.

As a result of the Letters of Administration, Rosamund and Hilda each received about £800. This was a sizeable amount, but not enough for them to live on indefinitely. Right up to her marriage in 1911, Rosamund is always described as 'of independent means', so I suspect that rather more substantial sums were passed to her by her father before his death, possibly to avoid Death Duties.

The sisters seemed to continue living together following Henry's death. For example, they took a trip to Malta together on the *S.S. Clan Mackenzie* from Liverpool in December 1894.

By the following year they were living at Thornby Hall in Northamptonshire, another grand house in the middle of the English countryside. By this time they both seemed to be active members of the Primrose League. This had been founded in 1883 to promulgate Conservative principles. It was named after the favourite flower of Benjamin Disraeli. It aimed at a mass membership and had two categories of member: full members, who paid an annual subscription of half a crown, and associates, who only paid a few pence. It aimed to attract working class members and gave women the same status and responsibilities as men. Membership rose quickly, reaching over one million by 1891, which was more than trade union membership at the time. By 1910, membership reached over two million, but after the First World War it declined rapidly.

The League had many social events organised for its members, culminating in summer fetes, held in the grounds of various stately homes.

I suspect that some time in early 1896 Rosamund moved to London and, as a result, she became, I think, more involved in the varied activity and interests which living in the capital provided. Certainly by late 1899 she was living at 18 York Street Chambers, Bryanston Square, West London.

These were built by the Ladies' Residential Chambers Company, which had been set up in 1888 by Agnes Garrett, sister of Elizabeth Garrett Anderson, the first woman doctor. The idea was to provide comfortable, purpose-built self-contained accommodation for educated working women in a safe environment.

Agnes had set up the first female design and decorating company in 1875, winning many prestigious interior decoration commissions from such individuals as the composer, Hubert Parry. She was also a strong supporter of women's suffrage.

Agnes started in 1889 with a successful project, the Chenies Street Chambers in Bloomsbury, which:

> ... catered for middle- and upper-class women working as doctors, artists and music teachers, who lived in individual bed-sitting rooms, with a shared dining room, which ensured the requisite privacy and decorum of their social class.[24]

The Chenies Street Chambers were clearly successful because in 1890, the architects Turner and Balfour had designed another set of chambers to be erected in York Street, Marylebone:

> This was not, at first glance, dissimilar to other mansion blocks in Marylebone although a stone plaque announced it as being exclusively for ladies. The 50 residents had a choice of flats (bedrooms with separate sitting rooms) or bed-sitting rooms, which were both relatively commodious arrangements. The basement had both private and large communal dining rooms as well as servants' rooms ostensibly providing housing for another less visible class of working women. These layouts suited an emerging class of professional women with a genteel balance of private accommodation that allowed for respectability and independence also with some communal spaces that fostered networking, support and camaraderie. Indeed the first women members of the RIBA (Royal Institute of British Architects), sisters Ethel and Bessie Charles, ran their architectural practice from here.[25]

---

[24] Emily Gee '"Where shall she live?" Housing the New Working Woman in Late Victorian and Edwardian London', in Geoff Brandwood (ed.), *Living, Leisure and Law: Eight Building Types in England 1800-1941* (Spire Books, in association with the Victorian Society, 2010) pp. 89-109.

[25] ibid.

Elizabeth Crawford gives further details:

The eventual layout of the York Street Chambers allowed for a greater flexibility in living arrangements, units included bedsitting rooms as well as bedrooms with separate sitting room and the tenants shared a pantry, than had Chenies Street. In the basement there was a large communal dining room as well as another for private dinners. The York Street Chambers was twice as expensive to build as Chenies Street. It is still a handsome building, both inside and out. Two wings sweep forward enclosing the entrance front and giving an illusion of shelter. The red brick is liberally laced with small-paned, white-painted sash windows and the skyline is marked by an array of pedimented dormers linked rhythmically by curvaceous brickwork. A shallow banding above the ground floor and a more elaborate, dentilled, cornice above the second storey breaks up the height of what is in fact a six-storey building. Inside the original, subtly shaded green tiles lining the corridors to dado height, the elegant columns in the entrance hall and the narrow sweep of the brass handrail up the stairs, give an indication of the care taken over the fitting out. The former dining room is still made decorative by the presence of its original cream, blue and green, rather 'Persian', tiles.[26]

She continues:

One of the early tenants was a young woman teaching at Bedford College, who later, as Molly Hughes, described in A London Home in the Nineties the thrill of sharing a tiny flat there with a colleague. 'We found a dignified Lady Superintendent, who informed us that every applicant must have references and must agree to certain regulations, of which the chief seemed to be that no nail must be driven into the walls. There was a flat available on the top floor, containing two rooms and a third little place, half kitchen, half scullery. One bathroom, charged extra,

---

[26] Elizabeth Crawford *Enterprising Women: The Garretts and their Circle* (Francis Boutle Publishers, 2002) p. 214.

had to serve all the flats on one floor. There were six stories and no lift. Well, it seemed to us the promised land, and we spent all our spare time figuring out the cost. The rent was high and we had no furniture, but we reckoned that in the long run we should spend less than in our lodgings, and get infinitely more comfort... Meals gave us no problem for a good dinner was served in the common dining-room ... [and] was always a pleasant interlude, for we met a variety of interesting women, all of them at work of some kind - artists, authors, political workers, and so on.[27]

It may have been that the rents in York Street were higher than in Chenies Street. Certainly the company appears to have found rooms there a little more difficult to let and in 1895 placed a series of advertisements in the Athenaeum, the Manchester Guardian, the Queen, and the Journal of Education. Alice Zimmern, herself a tenant in York Street, writing in the Contemporary Review in 1900 about the problem of accommodation for women, commented that because the rents of the flats owned by the Ladies' Residential Chambers were so high most of the tenants were either 'ladies of independent means, or such as supplement their professional income from private sources'. This description does appear to fit those living in York Street rather than those in Chenies Street, where, as we have seen, the directors were intent on maintaining their policy of letting to women who worked and were prepared to do what they could to help them. In 1903 it was agreed at one meeting of the directors that a notice about Swanley College should be posted in both sets of chambers and at another that they were happy for a doctor to put up a brass plate and practise from her rooms.[28]

The interchange of ideas that must have taken place in the communal areas with women of an intellectual character would certainly have introduced Rosamund to a variety of new movements and philosophies. Although Rosamund attended a

[27] ibid. p. 215.
[28] ibid.

Primrose League ball in Fulham Town Hall in February 1896, from then on there are no further reports of her interest in the League, which is perhaps one indication of her attention being turned to other things. Perhaps also it may be an indication that Hilda was the one who was the instigator of the half-sisters' activities in the Primrose League.

28. York Street Chambers, London

Rosamund does not appear in the 1901 Census, taken on 31st March that year. Her half-sister, Hilda, does not appear either and they may well have been travelling abroad together.

On 25th January 1902, Hilda married Captain Frederick Manners-Smith (1868-1914) of the 2nd Battalion, 3rd Goorkha Rifles, in India. It has been suggested that Rosamund was out of the country to attend Hilda's wedding, but this is unlikely because of the length of time she would have had to be away, her absence from the Passenger Lists for the period and, crucially, from an extensive newspaper account of the wedding, which does not mention her.

Nevertheless it is likely that Rosamund's absence from the Census was occasioned by her being abroad, probably on the continent of Europe. She was 36, probably missing her half-sister and of an age to be experiencing the so-called 'mid-life crisis'. A trip, either working or studying abroad or even undertaking the 'Grand Tour' must be considered at least a possibility.

8
The man with too many names

On 22nd May 1911, Rosamund, at the age of 46, got married to Thomas George Alford Broadfield Sabine. Or so it said on the marriage certificate, though I could find no record of the birth of anyone with that name.

As we shall subsequently see, he was, later in life, a member of an Irish regiment and I thought that it was the very incomplete Irish records which were to blame.

However, nothing was ever quite what it seemed with George (as he was known) and I began to suspect that at least one of his many names had been added later.

A Register taken in 1939 gave his date of birth as 15th February 1872, which was something to check likely birth records against.

An examination of birth records for the first quarter of 1872 gave a Thomas George Broadfield. I had a feeling that it would be worth spending £9.50 on sending for his Birth Certificate. When it arrived a few days later I opened the envelope in anticipation. Would it give the date of birth as 15th February, a 1 in 90 chance?

Yes, there it was! Thomas George Broadfield was born on 15th February 1872 at 59 Coleshill Buildings, Pimlico, in the County of Middlesex to Annie Millward Broadfield, formerly Adams, and Thomas Joseph Broadfield, whose occupation is given as musician. I had found him! On his marriage certificate, George had given his father as 'Thomas Joseph Sabine', just one of several deceptions!

Coleshill Buildings was a block of tenements in the south-west London district of Belgravia built by the Improved Industrial Dwellings Company on land owned by the Duke of Westminster, a major landowner in the area. This had been founded by Sir Sydney Waterlow, the printer, philanthropist and later Lord Mayor of London in 1863. Its policy was to provide dwellings for 'the labouring classes' whilst providing a reasonable dividend for the company's shareholders, the so-called "five percent philanthropy".

29. Coleshill Buildings, Pimlico, London

Living accommodation in London in the mid-19th Century was often extremely squalid with severe overcrowding. The Improved Industrial Dwellings Company was one of a number of companies and philanthropic bodies which were established in the latter half of the 19th Century to provide much better living accommodation, mostly self-contained flats, including an indoor toilet.

The very poor were excluded, however, because it was thought that they would be unable to pay the rents. However, it would seem as if George's parents were not in this category. I don't know what sort of musician Thomas Joseph Broadfield was, but the family were obviously able to afford the rent.

Coleshill Buildings were particularly lavish in detail. John Nelson Tarn remarks:

> *The neighbourhood being rather superior to the districts in which the company's tenements had been previously*

erected, and as the Marquis required the buildings to be made externally as attractive as possible, the directors had varied their general design of construction by the introduction of large shops with suitable accommodation for the shopkeepers on the ground floor, keeping all the upper storeys for small tenements, and had arranged high gable roofs in the fronts next to the main streets.[1]

He remarks elsewhere that:

[Coleshill Buildings] consisted of two splayed blocks at the junction of Ebury Road and Pimlico Road, each five storeys high and planned on the same principles as all the buildings in the past. The only innovation was the introduction of a new kind of 'patent stone' for lintels, stairs and other details, which, it was claimed, would result in a saving of 20 per cent on the total cost. The estate, with a total accommodation for 120 families, included ten shops, and was completed in November 1870.[2]

Tarn also remarks that:

... the Improved Industrial Dwellings Company was criticised for its policy, and accused of providing homes only for the superior artisan, rather than the poorer working man whose need was greatest.[3]

However, he points out:

... [Waterlow] determined to show that building working men's homes need not be unprofitable for commercial companies.... [He] proceeded with the venture privately because he wanted to prove to his more sceptical friends that his scheme was possible, and that they might safely invest their money in the company which he hoped to float.[4]

---

[1] John Nelson Tarn *Five Per Cent Philanthropy* (Cambridge University Press, 1973) p. 55.

[2] John Nelson Tarn - 'The Improved Industrial Dwellings Company' in *Transactions of the London and Middlesex Archaeological Society* Vol. 22 Part I (1968) pp. 43-59.

[3] ibid. p. 48.

[4] ibid. p. 46.

Waterlow himself summed it up thus:

All that I have endeavoured to show is that capital, expanded in the erection of light, cheerful, healthy habitations for the industrial classes in crowded cities, may be made to yield a fair interest on its investment, if care is taken to avoid extravagance in external architectural decoration or loss by large management expenses.[5]

George's father seems to have disappeared by 1877, in which year Annie marries Edward William Sabine, a wine and spirit valuer. By 1881 they are living at 80 Larches Street, Aston, a suburb of Birmingham.

On 6th January 1890, George Alfred Sabine (the "Alfred" had arrived from somewhere!) joined the First Royal Dragoons at Colchester. He later joined the Royal Inniskilling Fusiliers and on 21st August 1895 he was commissioned as 2nd Lieutenant into the 3rd (Reserve) Battalion. On 2nd January 1897 he was promoted to Lieutenant.

On 22nd December 1897, George was appointed to the newly-formed West African Frontier Force in Lagos, Nigeria. Haywood and Clarke write of the origins of this:

The story is told of a weary and exhausted traveller, riding a jaded horse across the uplands of Yorubaland in the middle of last century, surrounded by tribes making war upon each other for the purpose of capturing and selling slaves. As this man went through the country slaves ran away from their masters, seeking his protection. He reached Lagos in safety, and, on his return journey, these free slaves, organized and armed by him, gave him protection and encouraged others to join him. This man was Lieutenant Glover, R.N., later Sir John Glover, Governor of Lagos.... The slaves he had freed formed the

---

5 *The Times* 14 April 1863.

Lagos Constabulary and were known as 'Glover's Hausas'.
The year was 1863.[6]

When the West African Frontier Force was established in 1897 it *was a regular military force, recruited from a nucleus of officers and men of the Royal Nigerian Constabulary, supplemented by Regular Army officers and newly enlisted Hausas, Yorubas and Nupes.*[7]

George was one of those officers. The force was initially established because the British were concerned about French colonial expansion in the area. He was initially employed with the Lagos Constabulary.

On 1st July 1899, he was promoted to Captain. He was counted as an "Officer holding an Appointment not included in the Staff of the Army - Various".

On 26th March 1904 George was appointed Deputy Governor of Gaols, Southern Nigeria. This was, I imagine, a very taxing post, as by January 1905, he is absent from the Army Lists, having retired at the age of 33.

There is some evidence that his retirement at this relatively young age was due to what we might today call post-traumatic stress disorder. Also, he appears to have contracted malaria.

[6] Colonel A. Haywood and Brigadier F. A. S. Clarke *The History of the Royal West African Force* (Gale and Polden, 1964) p. 5.

[7] ibid p 31.

9
Vacuna in Sussex

To return to Rosamund, we know that by January 1900 she had been accepted as an Associate Member of the Society for Psychical Research. This had been formed in 1882. Its aims were "to examine without prejudice or prepossession and in a scientific spirit those faculties of man, real or supposed, which appear to be inexplicable in terms of any generally recognized hypotheses."

It was really the first organisation to look, in a sensible and relatively unprejudiced way, at all psychic phenomena, including telepathy, clairvoyance, psychometry; ghosts and poltergeist activity; and communication with the dead, amongst others.

At the time Rosamund joined, it largely consisted of middle-class intellectuals. The extent to which she was actively involved in attending meetings and carrying out research I have yet to discover.

In 1901, John M. Watkins opened his shop at 21 Cecil Court, off Charing Cross Road, in the heart of London. Regular visitors in the shop's early days included W.B. Yeats, poet and member of the Golden Dawn, and G.R.S. Mead, a prominent figure in the Theosophical Society. Just as it is today, even with the wealth of resources available on the internet, the presence of a specialist occult bookshop, with its knowledgeable staff and clientele, would have been an undoubted attraction for Rosamund, starting out on her esoteric studies. I visited it myself on a regular basis from the late 1950s.

Still a thriving shop to this day, Watkins' website includes more details of its history:

John Watkins was a friend and disciple of H.P. Blavatsky and was himself personally involved in seeing the first edition of The Secret Doctrine, her great metaphysical classic, through his printing press. The ideal of founding the bookshop is said to have occurred to Mr Watkins in a conversation with Madame Blavatsky in which she lamented the fact that there was nowhere in London one could buy books on mysticism, occultism and metaphysics.[1]

Most of the major figures in British occultism would have visited the shop, including such luminaries as MacGregor Mathers and Aleister Crowley.

Rosamund could well have been introduced to many of her life-long interests through visiting Watkins on a regular basis between 1901 and 1903 while she was living in London. Details of meetings and lectures on a variety of topics and by a variety of organisations would be displayed within the shop, and she may well have met A.E. Waite, who was a frequent visitor to Watkins and who founded the Rectified Rite, which Rosamund applied to join in 1905.

In April 1899, Rosamund had an article entitled 'The Cult of Physiognomy' published in *The Humanitarian*, a journal edited by Victoria Woodhull Martin (1838-1927), the first woman to run for President of the United States, and an activist for women's rights. She was the first female stockbroker. A newspaper which she owned with her husband had published the first English version of Karl Marx's 'Communist Manifesto' in 1871.

Victoria moved to England in 1877 and, with her husband, John Biddulph Martin, published *The Humanitarian* in England from 1892 to 1901. It was, to start with, largely concerned with eugenics, a term first used by Francis Galton in 1883, which is essentially about improving the genetic quality of humans. It has now been largely discredited.

---

[1] https://watkinsbooks.com/history

By 1897, *The Humanitarian* was being increasingly devoted to psychic studies and it was probably this element that attracted Rosamund's attention. She may well have felt that physiognomy had something to contribute to the themes covered by *The Humanitarian*.

Physiognomy is the assessment of a person's character by looking at their appearance, particularly the face. It was first developed as a practice by the ancient Greeks and was popularised in Europe by the Swiss writer, Johann Kaspar Lavater (1741-1801).

By the time Rosamund was writing her article, the practice was falling out of favour. It is clear, however, that she was not only knowledgeable on the subject but had developed her own distinctive approach.

Rosamund's article gives a general introduction to what she calls the cult of physiognomy ('cult' having a more positive connotation than is common nowadays, as we shall see in subsequent chapters). The article begins:

> *Every face is either a history or a prophecy; in age the former, in youth the latter. There is an instinctive physiognomy, much practised by dogs and children, who form an instant, unhesitating opinion on the merits or otherwise of any person presented to their notice for the first time. This instinct rarely errs, and is possessed by some fortunate adults under the name of intuition - a seeing into - the power of instantly perceiving the main points in a character without reasoning or analysis. Intuition is a gift of the gods. Much of the success of great leaders of men is due to this faculty of rapid judgement, of glancing for a moment into the secret souls of smaller folk and reading there the natural bent towards truth or falsehood. Such moments are like the lightning flash at midnight, unfolding heaven and earth - then darkness falls again, but what has been thus revealed, though only for an instant, remains a memory for ever.[2]*

---

2   R. Carnsew 'The Cult of Physiognomy' in *The Humanitarian* April 1899 pp. 263-272.

Rosamund follows the doctrine of astral influence on physiognomy as postulated by Jacob Boëhme (1576-1624), the German
philosopher, as opposed to Lavater's approach, which denied
such influence. However, she gives an outline of each system, for
she writes:

> *Physiognomy as a science is a different matter. It enables*
> *those to whom the priceless gift of intuition has been*
> *denied to read character by rules, and adds certainty and*
> *detail to the quickest insight. This science is divided into*
> *two branches - Physiognomy and Pathognomy. The first*
> *treats of the powers and inclinations of men - the second of*
> *the signs of the passions. One teaches how to observe*
> *character at rest, the other character in motion.*

Interestingly, she quotes Lavater in the original French, but does
not translate the quotations. I think perhaps she thought that all
educated people could read French and therefore she didn't need
to offer a translation.

Rosamund was well aware of the limited nature of the article, for
she ends it thus:

> *These short studies are the minutest pebbles picked up on*
> *the shore of the great science of Physiognomy. Perhaps this*
> *is somewhat at a discount, because it does not attempt to*
> *predict the fortunes of the subject, except so far as his*
> *natural disposition will affect his career. But the art of*
> *reading faces is useful, as well as interesting. Even a slight*
> *knowledge enables a student to guess something of a*
> *character, though the difficulty of forming an accurate*
> *judgement is often great to the most experienced professor.*
> *Lavater himself said that he daily met a hundred faces*
> *concerning which he could pronounce no certain opinion.*
> *In this world of dreams we are all such mysteries to one*
> *another that the closest friend is but as one who clasps our*
> *hand in the darkness. Physiognomy and its kindred*
> *sciences may help to lift the veil for a moment, for strange,*
> *unguessed-of secrets may be read by such means. Some*
> *souls are dumb, and cannot speak for themselves.*

The article does seem to indicate that Rosamund had an unusual interest in astrology in that she uses the minor planet Juno in her deliberations.

Now, this is interesting in that when Juno was first discovered it was thought to be a planet in its own right, almost ten times the diameter that more recent measurement has determined. Until about 1845, therefore, the four asteroids of Vesta, Juno, Ceres and Pallas were given planetary status by astrologers. After that date, however, their use fell away, only really coming into prominence in the 1980s, when ephemerides giving their accurate positions became available.

The above would suggest that Rosamund learnt her astrology from a book or books published before 1845 or from a tutor who learned their astrology from before that date. It is worth noting that Juno appears again in another context later in this chapter.

Perhaps the confidence which Rosamund must have gained through having an article published in *The Humanitarian* meant that she felt able to write other articles in the next few years. I have so far tracked down two, but there may well be more. One is entitled 'Haunted Roads' which appeared in *Temple Bar*, the same magazine in which her father's translation of Alfred de Vigny appeared some 23 years previously.[3] The other is a short story, 'Prudence and the Prince', which was published in *The London Magazine* in 1904.[4]

Although very different, these two pieces have in common a strong emphasis on Cornwall, a land in which both of Rosamund's parents had ancestry. Doubtless she would have made the railway trip from London to Cornwall fairly frequently with her grandparents from time to time to keep contact with those still living in the land which was their ancestral home.

---

3 R. Carnsew Haunted Roads in *Temple Bar* April 1903 pp 465-471.
4 R. Carnsew - Prudence and the Prince in *The London Magazine* (Harmsworth Magazine) No 13 August 1904-January 1905 pp. 284-289.

'Haunted Roads' does indeed cover roads said to be haunted, particularly those in Cornwall. The article gives no references, but I suspect that it is based on earlier works of Cornish folklore plus perhaps one or two accounts which were told to her.

The article includes a negative reference to witches (or is it?), which seems to demonstrate that she didn't consider herself one in 1903:

> The district [of Porthcurno] *has always been one of evil-omen; it is said that all the ills incident to man have been brewed by witches on the wild rocks about the Logan Stone; for there, from time immemorial, they have held their Sabbaths under the personal superintendence of their master the devil. There they initiate their neophytes with weird rites, the chief being that the aspirant to infernal honours must climb nine times on to the rocking stone, at midnight, without shaking it, a difficult gymnastic feat.*[5]

'Prudence and the Prince' is a short story set in an "old-world Cornish town". It concerns activities at a Whitsuntide fair:

> *Usually the clanging cry of the seabirds, coming and going with the tide in the estuary, and the musical trickle of clear water, flowing everywhere through deep gutters, were the chief sounds breaking the sleepy stillness of its grey streets. But during Whitsuntide it awoke. Then all was bustle, for this was fair time, the great event of the peaceful year. Cattle and sheep were penned in the broad market-place under the square towers of the ancient church. Stalls or booths covered with fairings, flowers, bowls of scald-cream, and cakes were protected by coloured awnings from the hot May sun. A genial gaiety, rather Continental than wholly English, inspired the occasion with liveliness.*[6]

Seventeen year old Prudence and her thirteen year old brother, Mark, bring their pony-driven cart to the fair, filled with produce.

---

[5]   'Haunted Roads' p. 468.
[6]   'Prudence and the Prince' p. 284.

In recording their conversation, Rosamund provides them both with a strong Cornish accent.

A performer of magic tricks, who was supposed to be a Russian prince exiled for his political opinions, turns out to be "a Romany lad, with a gift of shooting straight, by which he gets his living".[7]

> *He ... whispered words that fell meaningless on her childish ears. Even the broad, gold moon seemed to wear a new expression on her calm face, looking down upon this witches' revel. Prue, who usually saw her climb a dark hill-shoulder, flooding a lonely moor with light, vaguely feared this old acquaintance might be shocked. She had yet to learn that nothing can disturb the inscrutable composure of the moon.*[8]

Prudence was someone who struck him immediately as being different:

> *The fact that she sat still and contented struck him as remarkable. Most girls chattered and used their eyes when alone with a man. Then his gipsy instinct recognised that her short life had been lived between moor and sea, where human speech was superfluous.*

In her turn, she was rather swept off her feet by him and very quickly almost decided to go off and live with him. But her father found out and organised a special prayer-meeting on her behalf, where he "wrestled with the devil for her soul" until Prudence repented in a "burst of hysterical tears".

One wonders how much of this may be from Rosamund's own youth and whether her grandfather may have similarly tried to control her interests and liaisons.

———————————— ••■◆■•• ————————————

7   ibid. p. 285.
8   ibid. pp. 285-286.

The next we know of Rosamund is that she is living in the parish of Sutton in west Sussex, just north of the range of hills known as the South Downs. She appears for the first time in the 1904 electoral register as living at Sutton End, a small hamlet about a mile north of the village of Sutton. I have only recently checked the electoral registers. The street directories which I looked at previously merely gave her address as 'The Bungalow, Sutton' and I wrongly identified this as being a wooden bungalow on the southern edge of the village.[9] However, the electoral registers are much more specific and, on visiting Sutton End, I found only one building which matched the description of 'The Bungalow'. Indeed, in the 1911 Census, after Rosamund had left the village, that property in Sutton End is specifically referred to as 'The Bungalow'.

30. The Bungalow, Sutton End, West Sussex
Rosamund's home from 1903 to 1910

Interestingly, throughout her time in Sutton, Rosamund is referred to in the electoral registers as 'Rosanna'. This could just be a simple mistake in reading her application form by the registering officer, which was repeated from year to year, or it could represent a genuine, if limited, desire on Rosamund's part to start a new phase of her life with a new name, perhaps influenced by some knowledge of numerology.

---

[9] Heselton 2003 p. 71.

Mary K. Greer in her *Women of the Golden Dawn - Rebels and Priestesses* starts Chapter 24, entitled "Swept by a Tumultuous Power" with an evocative paragraph:

> *Early in 1903 a major hurricane swept through the British Isles, toppling ancient trees and destroying homes; many a landscape was permanently changed. It came to be known as the Year of the Great Wind. And for several of the Golden Dawn members, the hurricane seemed to reflect a time of death and rebirth in which the landscape of their lives was drastically reordered. Each was swept by an overwhelming force into a new order. The tumultuous power of their desires and emotions required new forms to contain them.*[10]

And 1903 was a pivotal year in Rosamund's occult development.

Sutton End is only about a mile from Burton Park, which I have already mentioned as having been the venue for the house party attended by Rosamund and Hilda back in 1891.

Burton Park had been a centre for Catholicism for centuries. Holt writes:

> *The house and estate, owned by the Gorings in the sixteenth century, passed in 1724 to the Biddulphs of Staffordshire and in 1835 from them to the Wrights of Essex. On inheriting the property, Anthony George Wright added Biddulph to his name.*[11]

Burton Park and the surrounding area seem to have remained a centre for Catholic activity well into the 20th Century. Well-known Catholic author, Hilaire Belloc, wrote his book *The Four Men: A Farrago*[12] about a walk the length of Sussex, while staying with the Wright-Biddulphs at Burton Park.

---

[10] Mary K. Greer *Women of the Golden Dawn - Rebels and Priestesses* (Park Street Press 1995) p. 274.

[11] T G Holt, 'Burton Park: A Centre of Recusancy in Sussex' in *Recusant History* Vol 13 (1975) pp. 106-122.

[12] Hilaire Belloc *The Four Men: A Farrago* (Thomas Nelson and Sons, 1911).

At some stage, George Sabine moved to Burton Common, less than a mile walk from Sutton End. As mentioned, he had retired from the Army at the very end of 1904, and we know he was living in Barlavington parish by 1905 as he is mentioned as being a resident in that year.

There is evidence, which I shall present shortly, to suggest that Rosamund knew, and had a close relationship with, George by May 1905 at the latest. So we have a short period of a few months, from the end of 1904 to April 1905, when George must have moved to Burton Common. Ultimately, we don't yet know how Rosamund and George first met. It could have been by chance walking along the lanes of that sparsely populated part of Sussex, or they could have met in London following George's retirement in 1904, with George coming to live near Rosamund, who had already established herself in the area the previous year.

We have already noted that Rosamund had had an article published in *The Humanitarian* in 1899. It therefore seems quite likely that she was a subscriber to that magazine and may have had her first introduction to the Golden Dawn by reading an illustrated article about the Golden Dawn Temple in Paris in the February 1900 issue entitled "Isis Worship in Paris. Conversations with the Hierophant Rameses and the High Priestess Anari".

However, an event occurred in 1905, on May Day no less, which is revealing in more ways than one. It was while looking through R.A. Gilbert's admirable reference work, *The Golden Dawn Companion*[13] that I spotted the name Rosamund Carnsew. It was an exciting moment! It was the first time that I had been able to link the woman that Doreen Valiente had referred to as 'Mother Sabine' with any sort of esoteric or occult activity or interest.

On 1st May 1905, a Miss Rosamund Carnsew applied to be a member of the Order of the M[orgen] R[othe], also known as the Independent and Rectified Order R.R. et A.C. (Rosae Rubae et Au-

---

[13]   R. A. Gilbert *The Golden Dawn Companion* (Aquarian, 1986) p. 170.

reae Crucis - the Red Rose and the Cross of Gold) or the Independent and Rectified Rite of the Golden Dawn.

We have come upon the Golden Dawn before, when looking at the life of Edith Woodford-Grimes in Chapter 2.

In 1900, the Golden Dawn split over Mathers' admission that the founding letters of the Order had been forged by Westcott. This was reinforced after 1903, when there was a schism between those who favoured the focus being on magical working and those for whom mysticism was most important. Those who favoured continuing the magical tradition left the Order and in 1903, R. W. Felkin established the Stella Matutina. The faction loyal to Mathers became the Alpha et Omega and remained under his leadership; J. W. Brodie-Innes succeeded upon Mathers' death in 1918.

The London Isis-Urania temple of the Golden Dawn was taken over by the mystically inclined Arthur Edward Waite (1857-1942). He had originally been a Roman Catholic, but started to explore the occult, joining the Golden Dawn in 1891. He eventually became dissatisfied with the magical aspects and encouraged members towards a more mystical approach. In 1901, the Order changed its name to the Hermetic Society of the Morgen Rothe and in 1904 constituted the Rectified Rite, the full title of which was 'The Holy Order of the G[olden] D[awn] under the obedience of the Independent and Rectified Rite'. However, it began to be greatly affected by internal feuds and in 1914 Waite closed it down.

I have found no further record of Rosamund's involvement with the Rectified Rite or even whether she was accepted into membership. She was never a member of Waite's Fellowship of the Rosy Cross, which was founded in 1915 as a replacement for the Rectified Rite.

However, the Rectified Rite was not really the sort of thing that a complete beginner would wish to join or even know about. So, how would Rosamund have been in a position to apply for membership of the Rectified Rite? I have an idea. It may well be wrong, but it is often the way things happen.

It may have been via a gentleman by the name of Marcus Worsley Blackden (1864-1934). He was an artist and may have come to Rosamund's attention by a series of articles in the *Theosophical Review*, the first of which appeared in 1902 about the Egyptian Book of the Dead.

Apart from the subject matter, he may have interested Rosamund because he had a family connection with her step-mother, Hilda Carnsew, whose maiden surname was Worsley. As Sally Davis points out, there was a *thicket of cousin-relationships between the Blackden, Cayley, Worsley, Hollond and Franklyn families. dating back to the early 19th Century*.[14]

As Hilda's father was Frederick Cayley Worsley, I strongly suspect a family connection, though I have so far not attempted to disentangle the "thicket".

Marcus Worsley Blackden (known as "Worsley") was initiated into the Hermetic Order of the Golden Dawn at the Isis-Urania temple on 27th August 1896 and initiated into its inner second order on 6th November 1897.

In 1901, he became very close to A.E. Waite and they were both initiated as Freemasons on 10th February 1902. On 10th April 1902 they were both made members of the Societas Rosicruciana in Anglia (S.R.I.A.), which had a link with the earliest days of the Golden Dawn.

In the period up to 1903, Waite and Blackden were among those running the Golden Dawn during a turbulent period.

Eventually a break-away group formally inaugurated The Independent and Rectified Rite on 7th November 1903. It was run by

---

[14] http://www.wrightanddavis.co.uk/GD/MWBYOUTH.htm

three individuals: Waite, Blackden and Rev. William Alexander Ayton.

From 1905 to 1909, meetings of the Independent and Rectified Rite were held at Blackden's house, 16 Allison Road, Acton, West London. He subsequently lived in Blackfield, Hampshire, on the edge of the New Forest, until his death in 1934.

I have not yet disentangled the family relationships which appear to link Marcus Worsley Blackden with Rosamund's step-mother. If such a connection can be demonstrated, it would provide a direct link between Rosamund and a central figure in the Rectified Rite.

On the application form to join the Rectified Rite, everyone had to give a sacramental name by which they would be known. Most of the applicants gave a Latin motto of some sort, but Rosamund was the only one of the 80 or so applicants[15] to give the name of a goddess: Vacuna. This suggests perhaps an unfamiliarity with the tradition, a willingness to avoid a conventional approach or that the name given was already important to her.

Vacuna was a Roman Sabine goddess. The Sabines were the ancient people of what is now central Italy and their religious practices influenced many Roman customs. Ovid and Horace describe Vacuna as a very early water goddess, whose cult was celebrated near Lake Cutilia, in Italy. She became a goddess of the waters and the forests and a goddess of victory, to whom the people offered sacrifices when their work was over and they were at rest. Our word 'vacation' is thought by some to come from this attribute of Vacuna.

Rosamund must have read at some point that Vacuna was a Sabine goddess and identified with that because she already had some sort of relationship with George Sabine.

---

[15] Gilbert (1986) pp. 170-175.

That was not sufficient for Rosamund, however. She was the sort of woman who would want to explore further and would have read what was available on Vacuna and the Sabines generally. Indeed, she may have visited Italy to carry out her own investigations.

The Sabines were a people who lived in the hills north of Rome in an area known as Sabinium, which forms parts of the present-day regions of Lazio, Umbria and Abruzzo.

There was a temple to Vacuna near Horace's villa at Tibur. Horace (65 BCE - 8CE) was one of the greatest Roman poets. The modern village of Vacone is probably on the site of this temple. The goddess is still celebrated in the village: the 'Sacra Vacunae'.

Close to the village is the mysterious sacred wood, the Pago:

> *This place represents something deep and ancestral for all the inhabitants and is still the scene of celebrations for the whole community.[16]*

In the course of her investigations, Rosamund would undoubtedly have come across the legend of the so-called 'Rape of the Sabine Women'. This has been the subject of many famous artists including Poussin, Rubens and Picasso. It dates from the very early days of Rome, traditionally founded by Romulus.

The early Romans were short of women. Requests for women to marry their men were rejected. So they organised a festival and invited all to attend, which many did. At a signal from Romulus, the men grabbed many of the Sabine women. The use of the word 'rape' is a translation of the Latin 'raptio', which more accurately means 'abduction'. After much conflict, the Sabines agreed to join Rome to form one nation.

There are many stories told about the Sabine women. One tells that they had become sterile. Raven Grimassi continues the story:

---

[16] http://www.sabina.it/luoghi/horace.html

The Sabines then went to give prayer and offerings to the goddess Juno. Juno spoke through the sound of the winds rustling the trees, and told them their women must willingly submit to intimacy with a goat in order for their fertility to be restored (the goat was one of Juno's sacred animals). Lacking the desire to do as Juno had decreed, the Sabines turned to the Etruscans who were famous for their occult knowledge. One of the Etruscan priests told them to bring a goat offering. He then slew the goat and offered it to Juno. The priest cut the hide into straps and had the women appear before him and bare themselves. Then the priest had each woman pass by him as he lashed her across the back and buttocks with the goat strap. The lash penetrated the skin and thus were the women joined in intimate contact with the goat. Juno's decree was thereby honored and fertility was restored to the Sabine women.[17]

The emphasis on Juno in Rosamund's article about physiognomy, suggests that she was aware of Juno's significance for the Sabine women.

In the collection of artefacts in the possession of the Doreen Valiente Foundation there are a few items that are said to date back to the New Forest Coven. One must be extremely cautious about such statements, since they must have come from Doreen Valiente, who must have heard them from Gerald Gardner, who very likely obtained them from Edith Woodford-Grimes. I think it likely that some of Rosamund's ritual materials and other possessions were obtained by Edith from Rosamund's husband, George, after Rosamund's own death in 1948.

Anyway, one such item is a scourge, the handle of which is made of two woods, one with a fine reticulated surface like snake skin and one which appears to be a pine of some sort.

The scourge has symbols, carved by pyrography, which are identical to those on the Staff, as illustrated in Mathers' edition of the

17 Raven Grimassi *The Witches' Craft - The Roots of Witchcraft and Magical Transformation* (Llewellyn, 2005) p. 155.

Key of Solomon.[18] At the end of the handle is a silver cap, which has a hallmark which confirms that it was made in Birmingham in 1896. Attached to the other end of the handle are eight 'strings' of plaited wool.

I imagine that the (possibly) snake-skin covered handle was originally part of a silver-topped cane or swagger stick dating from 1896 and that at a later stage it was shortened and linked to a (possibly pre-existing) staff which had Solomonic characters already marked on it. It was joined to the remains of the cane by a patterned silver band which has a pentagram engraved on it.

The third element is the eight strings plaited from individual strands of wool, each of which has two or three knots along its length.

The whole handle has been stained a dark green and the strings are in blue and red.

I have no further reasons for linking this scourge to Rosamund, and indeed Gerald Gardner had several of these silver-topped canes, so it could have been made from a stick originally owned by him, which had been amended to include the Mathers symbols and, at a later date, its conversion into a scourge.

———————————— •-➖◆➖•• ————————————

Rosamund certainly continued her interest in magic and the occult because 25 years later there appeared an article in *The Occult Review* by one R. Sabine, entitled 'Rose of the World'.[19]

Her name, Rosamund, does, of course, mean " Rose of the World". Yet it took her over 30 years since her interest in the occult began, to write about the symbolic significance of the rose. She starts triumphantly:

---

[18] S. Liddell MacGregor Mathers *The Key of Solomon the King* (George Redway, 1888)

[19] R. Sabine 'Rose of the World' in *The Occult Review* Vol 52 August 1930 pp. 107-110.

This wondrous Rose is perhaps more comprehensive than any other occult symbol, and to fully understand it would be to know the meaning of the Universe.[20]

Rosamund goes on to liken the twelve outer petals of the mystic Rose to the signs of the zodiac and to the twelve single letters of the Hebrew alphabet.

She then likens the seven petals in the second circle of the Rose with the seven traditional planets, to the seven double letters of the Hebrew alphabet, and the many other correspondences of the number seven.

Evidence of her continuing interest in parapsychology and, indeed, of psychology itself, is given by her statement that:

Psychology is now an accepted science. Telepathy, clairvoyance and other kindred subjects are established facts. Psycho-analysis, hypnotism, suggestion are recognised methods of medical treatment. Everywhere the bounds of the material approach, or come into actual contact with, the psychic or astral plane.[21]

Rosamund then looks at the smallest, innermost circle of petals. These are three in number and correspond with the three elements of fire, water and air and the three mother letters of the Hebrew alphabet. She explains the absence of earth by saying that earth was "… not truly one element, but a compound of the other three."

She finishes the article:

In the heart of the Rose is the place of holiness. This is the centre of life, the dwelling-place of the One who is the source of all things, who manifests throughout the Universe. He is incomprehensible to us, only to be expressed by silence.

---

[20] ibid p 107.
[21] ibid p 108.

Gareth Medway commented to me that such an article at that date *must be by an initiate, so she must have gained admission to some branch of the Golden Dawn.*[22] R.A. Gilbert told me that *...she clearly was familiar with the Golden Dawn form which suggests that she had entered one branch of the original Order; probably Waite's, but possibly one of the others.*[23] And Alan Thorogood drew my attention to the fact that much of the article paraphrases elements of the Golden Dawn's ritual of initiation to the 1=10 grade of Zelator.[24]

The Occult Review was a well-respected journal in its field and to have an article published in it shows a certain degree of confidence in one's own knowledge and also confidence on the part of the editor. Of course, this is what one would expect from someone who had likely been involved in occult matters for at least the previous 30 years.

I think that this article helped to form the basis of the "rose group" which is discussed in Chapter 20.

---

[22] Gareth Medway - letter to the author 15 July 2002.
[23] R. A. Gilbert - letter to the author 6 March 2003.
[24] Alan Thorogood Personal communication with the author.

10

From Sussex to Dorset

In the 1911 Census, shortly before his marriage to Rosamund, George and his mother are recorded as living at Burton Common in the parish of Barlavington in Sussex. I do not know exactly where this is but, judging from the order in which the enumerator did their rounds, it would probably be close to Burton Park Road and not far from Burton Mill and Burton Hill. There is a low ridge of greensand sandstone which runs roughly east-west through the various parishes in the area and such places as Lavington Common, Duncton Common and Coates Common are all on this ridge, so it is reasonable to suppose that Burton Common is also, although I have not been able to find it on any map.

Perhaps Burton Common was in fact the name of a house, as it is not mentioned in any other context. Indeed, following her marriage in 1911, Rosamund's address, which the previous year had been given as "Bungalow, Sutton, Pulborough" was now "Burton Common, Petworth, Sussex", but still under her maiden name. It looks as if she moved in with George and his mother immediately following her marriage, but did not immediately change her surname to Sabine, though she did later.

I think it at least possible that, following his retirement in 1904, George spent some time at or in association with the Jesuit sanatorium at Burton Hill. The house was left to the Jesuits in about 1901 and whilst it was primarily intended for "Fathers and Brothers of Ours", i.e. Jesuits, a few laymen were admitted, and I suspect that George may have been amongst them.

Neither the Donnithornes nor the Carnsews were Catholics, and nor were the Broadfields or the Sabines, so it is unlikely that

George was brought up as a Catholic. He may, however, have converted at a later date. The lack of any known family connection with the Catholic Church suggests that any link with it on the part of Rosamund and/or George is likely to have occurred subsequent to their move to the Burton Park area, and perhaps as a result of Rosamund's earlier friendship with the Wright-Biddulphs.

In their wills they both requested that their bodies be cremated and, in addition, George requested that his ashes be scattered in a Garden of Remembrance. Now, the Catholic Church placed an official ban on cremation in 1886, which was not lifted until 1963. Between those dates the practice was strictly forbidden. Interestingly, the objection seemed to be, at least in part, that it was associated with what were seen as anti-Catholic organisations, particularly Freemasonry. The scattering of ashes was seen as particularly undesirable.

At any rate, the environment in that part of west Sussex, in the shadow of the South Downs, would prove conducive to recuperation after the undoubted trials and horrors of being in charge of prisons in Nigeria, as this account from 1922 makes clear:

> *The late donor, Charles Willcock, who afterwards assumed the name of Dawes ... bought Burton Hill, then part of the Park, from the owner, Squire Biddulph. ... Hereon he built a house for himself, the present building, and laid out the grounds with considerable skill and with an eye for beauty as well as comfort ...*

> *... The house, as the name implies, is built upon a slight eminence, and is protected from east winds by a belt of pine trees at a little distance, and a line of beautiful lime trees as the edge of the tennis lawn. In front, across an open stretch of Burton Park, almost a valley, a fine view of the Southern Downs ... is obtained. The land attached to the house, eighteen acres in extent, situated chiefly to the west and rear of the house, is surrounded by a narrow plantation of trees of many kinds, affording a shady and pleasant walk: but in wet and stormy weather a covered,*

open, ambulacrum adjoining the house supplies the need of those who require exercise, and two revolvable summer-houses are at the service of those who would wish to derive the full benefit of open-air treatment. There is stabling accommodation for eight horses, and the loft above is converted into bedrooms in case of need. Near the house is a walled kitchen garden and several greenhouses, wherein peaches, grapes and tomatoes flourish. On the front lawn are magnificent trees: oaks and pines, two fine cedars: one Canadian and the other Himalayan: and several Wellingtonias from Australia.

Burton Park ... is still accessible and is as delightful and varied in its aspects as could be wished. It covers an area of more than two thousand acres, and is stocked with fallow deer. In spite of the denudings of war-time, there are still many fine avenues of trees and forest-clumps. There are three natural ponds, two of which are secluded and abound in fish, while on the surface, mallards, coots and water-hens disport themselves. It is delightful on a sunny day to walk through the wooded dell and drink in the delicate aroma of the pine trees; or watch the gambols of the red squirrel; or listen to the cawing of rooks ... Besides the Park, there are many other equally attractive walks round about; for here we are in the heart of the country and fifty miles from London town.

One may sit at night with open window and listen to the deer barking in the park, or the croc of the pheasant disturbed by some nocturnal marauder ... All this tends to make the rest-cure more complete, for man never tends to be so physically fit as when he is in harmony with the great world of nature.

The house has more than justified its existence. More than a thousand in all ... have enjoyed in turn the benefit of the wholesome air ... The library is well stocked, but to the true lover of nature, the trees, the fauna, and the flowers, offer greater attractions.[1]

---

[1]   *Letters and Notices* Vol 37 1922 pp. 16-18.

The presence of stables at Burton Hill was probably taken advantage of by George, who doubtless learned to ride while he was in the Army in Africa. He certainly seemed to have made the acquaintance of Lord Leconfield's Hunt, based at Petworth House, only some two miles from Burton Hill. In the December 1927 issue of the *Sussex County Magazine* is a moving article by George entitled 'A Run with Lord Leconfield's Hounds'.[2] He starts vividly:

That a southerly wind and a cloudy sky proclaim a hunting morning is no longer accepted as infallible. Scent is as great a mystery as it was a century ago. Only the hound could offer any explanation on the subject, and he, unfortunately, cannot air his views with pen and ink. One thing is certain, that stormy weather is bad for chances of sport. Hounds are always wild, horses fidgety, and men consequently fractious on a windy day.

To look from the window and see great clouds racing across the sky before a strong sea-breeze blowing over the Downs, with gleams of sun, and spurts of rain between, however admirable as a landscape effect, is not reassuring as to hunting prospects.

Sussex has not the reputation of the Shires, but, on the other hand, it is free from overcrowding, the immense fields of the Midlands being quite unknown.

For those who cannot afford to pay fortunes for horses which really can gallop and jump, a second-rate country has many advantages. Among hills, dales and big coverts the pace is seldom tremendous, never for long at a time. Anyone who knows the country, mounted on a clever cob, can see everything and not have the annoying experience, like a bad dream, of seeing hounds vanish farther and farther away because only a thorough-bred can keep up with them.[3]

---

[2]   Major T. G. Sabine - 'A Run with Lord Leconfield's Hounds' in *Sussex County Magazine* Vol 1 December 1927 pp. 591-592.

[3]   ibid p. 591.

The Chichester Observer, in reviewing the piece, says that it is "very finely written":

> *One gets all the thrill of the chase in this, and even if one is not a huntsman, one can understand and feel in sympathy with every word.*[4]

I suspect that this article had been written when George was in Sussex before the First World War, and that he took advantage of the newly-published *Sussex County Magazine* to finally get it in print.

Another of George's long-standing interests was that of pony racing. Ponies are defined as being less than 15 hands and one of the earliest pony racing clubs was at Petworth. Known as the Lord Leconfield Branch of the Pony Club, it covers the area between Petworth and Billingshurst.

The Pony Club was founded in 1929. Before that was the Pony Turf Club, of which George was a Racing Steward.

In the 1911 Census, George's mother is indicated as being a widow. In fact, Edward William Sabine did not die until the following year, so I suspect that the couple had separated at some stage. George's mother had what one might call very flexible personal names. Her first names are given as 'Annie Millward' at her marriage in 1871 and on George's birth certificate in 1872. On her marriage to Edward William Sabine in 1877, her name is given as 'Annie Marian Adams', in other words reverting to her maiden name and changing her middle name. One can speculate the reasons for this, but I suspect that it could be because her first husband, Thomas Joseph Broadfield, was still alive (I have failed to find a death record for anyone of that name) and she did not want to be traced. By 1901 she had settled on 'Mary Ann', which remained her chosen name for the rest of her life.

---

4   Chichester Observer 7 December 1927.

On 22nd May 1911, Rosamund and George were married in the Catholic Church of Saints Anthony and George at Burton Park "according to the Rites and Ceremonies of the Roman Catholics", in the words of their marriage certificate.

It is interesting to note that George's middle name of Alfred has mysteriously been transformed to Alford, which is a name he kept for the rest of his life.

The clue as to what might have happened was provided by my friend from Somerset, Dave Holley, who, when talking to me about Albert Avenue in Hull referred to it as 'Allbert Avenue', and I now suspect that George pronounced his middle name as 'All-fred' to the registrar, who then incorrectly wrote it as 'Alford' in the register, having heard the name wrongly. George probably didn't like to correct the registrar, didn't notice it at the time, or thought it sounded good.

Indeed, Alford is not unknown as a personal name. In the two hours since writing the above I have come across two examples at random while doing other things!

George had been retired for some nine years when the First World War started in August 1914. He was caught up in the general enthusiasm and enlisted as a Temporary Captain in the Empire Battalion of the Royal Fusiliers (City of London) Regiment on 25th September 1914. However, only just over a month later, on 4th November 1914, he relinquished his temporary commission.

On 1st January 1915, he was appointed as an adjutant and temporary Captain in the 8th (Reserve) Battalion The Duke of Edinburgh's (Wiltshire Regiment). An adjutant is an administrative assistant to a senior officer. On 4th December that year he was promoted to Temporary Major.

The 8th (Reserve) Battalion was formed from volunteers at Weymouth in Dorset in November 1914 and moved to Trowbridge in Wiltshire in 1915. It was originally a Service Battalion but was converted to a Reserve Battalion in April 1915 and the following month moved to Wareham in Dorset. In September 1916 the battalion was absorbed into the Training Reserve Battalions of the 8th Reserve Brigade at Wareham. The battalion was never deployed overseas.

In 1917 and 1918, George seems to have been attached as a Major to either the 1st or 2nd Battalion of The Duke of Edinburgh's (Wiltshire Regiment). His Silver War Badge Roll indicates no particular action in that respect, although both battalions were deployed in France during that period and were involved in much military action.

George was 42 when the war started and it is my guess that he was somewhat protected in the roles he was given in the Army. His age and, I suspect, his fragile mental condition were such that he was given more of a training role than active service, the post of adjutant being a good example. Anyway, he seems to have retired permanently at the cessation of hostilities in November 1918.

Shortly after her marriage in 1911, we find Rosamund living at Llanteems Lodge, Llanvihangel Crucorney near Abergavenny in Wales. This seems to be another example of living somewhere fairly remote without any known connection with the local area. This is reminiscent of her father's occupation of Treago Castle in Herefordshire, which in fact is only some ten miles away. Perhaps Rosamund remembered with affection the landscape of the Welsh borders and chose to live there again when she could.

I don't know where Rosamund was living during the First World War, but it was probably close to Weymouth, or later Wareham, both in Dorset, where George was based.

Indeed it could have been in West Lulworth, a village some 15 miles from Weymouth and even nearer to Wareham, close to the coastal tourist attraction of Lulworth Cove. She and George were certainly living there, along with George's mother, in 1921-1922 in Churchfield House, West Road, West Lulworth, which is 400 years old and which had formerly been the Red Lion public house, which was visited by King George III in 1802.

31. Churchfield House, West Lulworth, Dorset

The end of the war meant that the Sabines had no particular reason to continue to live at West Lulworth. They wanted a bigger house, but why they chose Highcliffe, near Christchurch, on the Hampshire coast, I really don't know. But it is the village in which the origins of what Gerald Gardner called "the witch cult" are to be found, as we shall see in the next chapter.

.

11

Highcliffe - Wellspring of the Wica

Highcliffe-on-Sea is, as its name implies, a village on the south coast of England situated between the towns of Christchurch and Lymington in the historic county of Hampshire. It takes its name from the high cliffs which characterise the coast at this point but it is actually a relatively recent name. Until the beginning of the 19th Century it was largely open farmland, with the nearest settlements being at Chewton and Walkford. There was also a group of cottages at Slop Pond on the main Christchurch to Lymington road. Further houses were built here in the 1830s and the residents decided on a change of name to Newtown. It gained its own church, St. Mark's, in 1843. Development continued and at the turn of the 20th Century the name was again changed, this time to Highcliff. The 'e' at the end seems to have gained in popularity as the century progressed.[1]

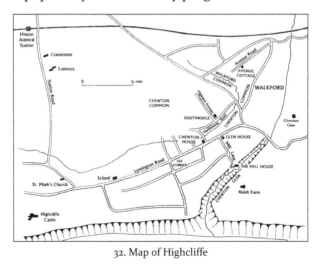

32. Map of Highcliffe

[1]   Sheila D. Herringshaw *A Portrait of Highcliffe* (Sheila D Herringshaw, 1981).

Highcliffe Castle, the local 'stately home', is really a series of gradual accretions to an older building, but is mostly 19th Century, although incorporating ancient stonework from France.

Highcliffe expanded greatly during the 1920s and 30s as part of the growth of Bournemouth and other seaside locations, being particularly popular with retired people. It is on the fringe of the New Forest and on the coast with magnificent views of the Isle of Wight so was, and still is, considered a desirable place to live.

To be honest, it is now more of a suburb than a village, yet behind its conventional façade something quite remarkable happened. It acted as a crucible for the modern pagan witchcraft revival. It was here that 'the witch cult', which grew into what we now know as Wicca, was born.

It makes one wonder whether Gerald Gardner's choice of Highcliffe to spend the early years of his retirement was a matter of chance. Indeed, I do suggest another possibility in Chapter 22.

We have already noted Hilaire Belloc's *The Four Men*, which was largely written at Burton Park. I now present 'The Four Women' who, as residents of Highcliffe and the vicinity formed the crucible from which the modern witchcraft revival emerged. They were Rosamund Sabine, Catherine Chalk, Katherine Oldmeadow and Dorothy Clutterbuck.

Dorothy is mentioned in *Gerald Gardner Witch*[2] and her identity was confirmed by the research carried out by Doreen Valiente, as I have already mentioned.

Doreen's marginal note in her own copy of that same book started me on my own investigations into Rosamund, which form the basis of Chapter 7.

My inclusion of the other two women, Katherine Oldmeadow and Catherine Chalk, is more speculative on my part but there is con-

---

[2]   op. cit.

siderable circumstantial evidence that they were part of a quartet of women who not only knew each other but were involved in various esoteric enterprises, including witchcraft.

These 'mothers of the Wica' were all from outside the area, but for some reason chose to settle down in Highcliffe. As Gareth Medway says:

One thing that continues to puzzle me is why there were so many occultists of various kinds in the Christchurch area in the 1930s. Within a few miles there were astrologers, spiritual healers, the Rosicrucians, the Order of Melchizedek, a Spiritualist Mission, Christian Scientists, and a Witch coven. Was this sheer coincidence? Did they settle there because the atmosphere was relatively friendly? Or was this ordained by the Gods, with the intention that a movement that began there would spread?[3]

Highcliffe in particular was, and remains, a place for people to retire to and, in our investigations, we have found the Clutterbucks, the Sabines and the Chalks finding the area suitable for that purpose.

We have already seen that Dafo and the Mason family started attending meetings of the Rosicrucian Crotona Fellowship in Christchurch by mid 1935. Bracelin writes of Gerald:

He found that his friends, after following Mabs to her settlement, had discovered an old Coven, and remained here because of that.[4]

Gerald himself said:

I found that Old Dorothy and some like her, plus a number of New Forest people, had kept the light shining.[5]

The phrase "discovered an old Coven" is an intriguing one. Whether Edith and the Mason family considered themselves

---

3   Letter from Gareth Medway to the author received February 2000.
4   Bracelin p. 166.
5   ibid.

witches before that encounter is a matter for further investigation, but it is clear that they considered that, by the use of the word "coven", they had met some who did consider themselves witches.

So who were they? Gardner mentions 'Old Dorothy' in this context and he obviously told Doreen Valiente that 'Mother Sabine' was a member of the coven. The use of the descriptions of the individuals as 'Old' and 'Mother' suggests to me that we are dealing with something well-established, as the use of the phrase 'old coven' would reinforce. We have already identified the individuals concerned as Dorothy Clutterbuck and Rosamund Sabine.

Where would Edith and the Masons have encountered members of the 'old coven'? They were travelling the 25 miles from Southampton to Christchurch for evening and occasional weekend meetings of the Crotona Fellowship, travelling by train or, more likely, bus, since it would have passed close to the Theatre, going home every night. Although latterly Edith moved to Christchurch and bought a house in nearby Dennistoun Avenue, and, even later, Susie Mason moved to Barrack Road in Christchurch, Ernie Mason, his mother and his sister, Rosetta, stayed in Southampton.

I have come to the conclusion that there is one, and only one, way in which Edith and the Masons could have met members of an old coven and that is via the activities of the Crotona Fellowship.

But did Dorothy and Rosamund have any connection with the Crotona Fellowship?

We will look at Dorothy's personality in Chapter 13, but I can say now that I have found no evidence to suggest any connection. I mention there that she did not seem to share the same esoteric interests and, moreover, there is never any mention of her as a performer in any of the Crotona Fellowship plays which were put on at the Ashrama, the Garden Theatre, or elsewhere. Knowing her personality, I can say that she would never have been content with being on the sidelines and would insist on a central part. She would definitely never have got on with Sullivan, and I am sure that if she ever did attend she would very quickly have left in a huff!

With Rosamund the reverse is true. In my view, it would be most unlikely if she had not made a connection with members of the Crotona Fellowship. She had lived in the area for about eleven years when the Ashrama was established at Meadow Way in 1935, plenty of time to make contact with individuals locally who were interested in the occult, some of whom at least would have let her know about this new activity going on only three miles from her house.

And it is likely that Rosicrucianism would have particularly interested Rosamund, since only five years previously she had had an article published in the Occult Review entitled 'Rose of the World, which, of course, is what her name means.

Indeed, Rosamund may have known Catherine Chalk prior to the establishment of the headquarters of the Crotona Fellowship at Meadow Way. To start with, they were almost exactly the same age, but crucially both had close relatives who married into the Wilde family. Catherine's aunt, Emily Chapman married Thomas Montague Carrington Wilde (1818-1878) in 1853. His nephew, Edward Archer Wilde (1826-1889) married Mary Penelope Donnithorne (1840-1918), Rosamund's aunt, in 1858. This was pointed out to me by Mary Kay Mahoney.

Incidentally, Edward's brother, James Plaisted Wilde (1816-1899), became the first and last Baron Penzance. Interestingly, his two interests were rose-breeding and championing the idea that Francis Bacon was the author of the works usually attributed to William Shakespeare, both of which have become familiar themes in the course of my researches.

Lucy Caroline Bevan was staying with Edward and Mary Wilde at their house in Eltham, Kent in 1871. She also witnessed the marriage certificate of Rosamund's parents in 1864. And Rosamund was staying with the Wildes in their house at 84 Lexham Gardens, Kensington immediately before her wedding in 1911.

The Donnithornes, Wildes and Stringers were all reasonably well-to-do families with, in some cases, substantial properties.

I cannot prove it, but it seems to me likely that Rosamund and Catherine knew each other from childhood and were even close friends. Certainly in later years they both had an interest in occult and esoteric matters.

Of the two families it was the Sabines who were the first to move into the area. They moved to 'Whinchat', a house at the junction of Avenue Road and Chewton Farm Road in Walkford.

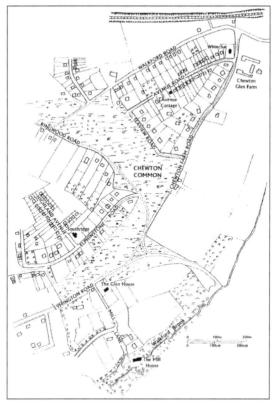

33. Highcliffe, Walkford and Chewton Common
(Based on the 1939 Ordnance Survey map)

There are no known photographs of 'Whinchat', but Ian Stevenson, the local historian in Highcliffe, tells me:

> *The Sabines' house was much more substantial* [than the bungalow currently on the site] *and when it was demolished, not only the Whinchat bungalow but at least two homes were built in its grounds. One is no. 1a Avenue Road and another fronts onto Chewton Farm Road ... the original garden was quite big ... and probably fairly secluded.*[6]

A notice appeared in the *Western Gazette* (North, South and West Dorset edition) for Friday 28th December 1923 which states:

> *Sale. Wednesday January 9th. Whinchat, Walkford, Highcliffe-on-Sea. Hewitt & Co., in consequence of their having sold the property will sell by auction the household furniture and Effects.*

We can therefore assume that the Sabines bought 'Whinchat' some time in late 1923 but did not move in until the sale of household effects had taken place and the purchasers thereof had removed them from the premises, let us say late January 1924.

Incidentally, the fact that the sale advertisement calls the house 'Whinchat' disproves my earlier suggestion that it had been thus named by the Sabines as containing the word 'Wica' if one looks at alternate letters.[7]

We shall examine the clues to the Sabines' involvement in 'the witch cult' shortly, but we shall first look at their life in Highcliffe and the wider context as a retired couple from 1924 onwards for the next 25 years or so.

And it is clear that this involvement, insofar as it existed, was by George rather than by Rosamund who, it seems, rarely appeared in public, perhaps echoing her great-aunt Eliza, being a bit of a

---

6   Letter from Ian Stevenson to the author 13 November 2000.
7   Philip Heselton (2003) p. 73.

recluse, or perhaps she may to some extent have been disabled and found it difficult to go out.

In October 1928, an indication of George's mental problems was given in at least two local papers. *The Christchurch Times*, under the heading of 'A Major's Lapse' published the following:

> *Major Thomas George Alford Broadfield Sabine (54), of Walkford, who had been remanded for a medical report, appeared before Mr. Fry, a London magistrate, this week, charged with obtaining at the Royal Automobile Club, Pall Mall, sums of £1 18s. 2d. and £2 by means of worthless cheques from Mr. Albert William Boast.*
>
> *Mr. H.R. Briant said that Major Sabine was formerly a member of the R.A.C. Last month he went to the club and on two successive days obtained from a waiter cheque forms which he filled in and cashed. If Major Sabine had not personally reported the matter to the police it was probable (added Mr. Briant) that the club would not have prosecuted.*
>
> *Detective-Sergt. Hawkes said Major Sabine had a most excellent record. He was educated at Trinity College, Dublin, and was gazetted to the Inniskilling Fusiliers.*
>
> *The magistrate said that the medical officer had reported that Major Sabine suffered from nervous instability, malaria, sunstroke and was abnormally sensitive to alcohol. This was probably the explanation of the case and he bound him over.*[8]

However, I enquired of Trinity College, which had no record of him ever being a student. This is, perhaps, another indication of his character.

An indication of George's reluctance to spend money is given in a letter he wrote to the local paper:

---

[8]   *Christchurch Times* 20 October 1928.

Now that the parish of Highcliffe has been absorbed into and become a ward of the Borough of Christchurch, the ratepayers having elected their councillors to serve their interests on the Borough Council, I beg to suggest that ratepayers of Highcliffe now form a Highcliffe and Walkford Ratepayers' Association, to watch their own interests.

Newly created and recently elected Borough Councils are, as history shows, inclined to justify their existence by a system of extravagance. History also shows it is quite an easy matter for Borough Councils to spend the ratepayers' money, unless a careful watch is placed on their activities, in that direction. Certain improvements are without a doubt necessary in Highcliffe. I note one of the councillor's election address contains the words "Progress and Economy". Let us, as ratepayers, see that we get the economy - the progress will and must proceed. The ratepayers as a whole must look to it that the economy also proceeds with the progress.[9]

A long-term inhabitant of Highcliffe, Gurth Brooke, remembered George:

I recall him round about the time of the start of the Second World War. ... He was regarded, quite frankly, as rather a flawed character. He always seemed to be in financial difficulties. In those days Lymington Road was a 'nation of shopkeepers' and he was rather a bogey-man with them, owing money all round, which was worse than murder in a community of shopkeepers. It was the most dreadful thing of all.

I remember when the Home Guard was formed in 1940, he came along and joined it, turning up in some kind of uniform wearing a tartan glengarry thing [it was actually a Balmoral bonnet]. *I think the age limit for the Home Guard was 65 or something like that, and Sabine would have been considerably more* [he was actually 68] *so his*

9   *Christchurch Times* 30 April 1932.

*association with it was very short and he just faded out. ...
He didn't serve with the Home Guard for any length of
time.*

*He was, so far as I recall, fair-haired, rather portly, a
typical senior military figure. He was, I'll say, not quite a
genuine character, and he was inclined to blow his own
trumpet a bit, and possibly make more of himself than he
was.*[10]

But was George in any way involved in the witch cult? Gerald
Gardner provides a clue when he writes:

*Now the god is represented by the high priest (if there is
one) and it is he who was called the Devil in the old days. I
was very curious about him and asked at once when I was
"inside", by which they mean a member of the cult: "Who
and what is called the Devil?" Though members of the cult
never use and, indeed, dislike the term, they knew what I
meant and said: "You know him, the leader. He is the high
priest, the high priestess's husband."*[11]

Now, if we take this statement at face value, it means that Gardner knew the high priest, who was married to the high priestess.
Dafo was separated from her husband; Dorothy's husband had
died in May 1939; Catherine Chalk's husband had died in 1931 and
Irene Lyon Clark's in 1934; Ernie and Susie Mason, Katherine
Oldmeadow and Elsie Begg had never married. There is one, and
only one, married couple who have been suggested as being in the
witch cult and they are George and Rosamund Sabine.

———————————— ·•━◆━•· ————————————

The Chalks came to Somerford in about 1925, probably the year
after the Sabines moved to Walkford. An obituary of Thomas
Chalk which appeared in the *Christchurch Times* in 1931 talks of
their "taking up residence here some six years ago", in other

---

[10] Gurth Brooke - interview with Ian Stevenson 19 November 2004.
[11] Gardner (1954) pp. 130-131.

words about 1925. They appear in the electoral register for the first time in 1926, which is consistent with arriving some time in 1925.

The Chalks must have contemplated moving to the area in early 1924, since they had plans for a substantial two-storey house drawn up by August 1924. Given time for the house to be built also brings us to a 1925 date for moving in. This house became known as Meadow Way, in the grounds of which were subsequently built the Ashrama and the Garden Theatre.

12

Herbs and a Herbalist

I think it is reasonable to assume that Doreen's marginal note about 'Mother Sabine' was as a result of information obtained from Gerald Gardner, though she was also in touch with Edith Woodford-Grimes and perhaps others who would have known Rosamund.

Gardner also refers to 'Mother Sabine' in another context - a letter he wrote to Cecil Williamson in December 1953. He writes:

> *Old Mother Sabine died recently & Ive got her very nice little cabinet of little draws & lots of little Boxes & things etc. but the Herbs have mostly mouldered away. It smells wonderful though, & there's an Old Culpepper with 1684 Original binding.[1]*

The reference to a Culpeper volume of 1684 is interesting, as Gerald Gardner ended up with that very volume in his library. Its title was The English Physician enlarged with 369 Medicines made of English Herbs, first published in 1652.

Now, it is interesting to note that Rosamund died in May 1948, over five years before Gardner is writing "Old Mother Sabine died recently." I think the explanation for this may be that he had not had any direct contact with Rosamund for several years and that after he moved away from Highcliffe in 1945, I suspect that his only contact with the witch cult and with Highcliffe generally was Edith and that any local news was filtered through her.

George survived Rosamund by over two years until he died in December 1950. At the time he was living in a nursing home and I

---

[1] Letter Gerald Gardner to Cecil Williamson 23 December 1953 - Document 89 - Boscastle Museum of Witchcraft.

imagine that Whinchat was probably sold shortly after Rosamund died. If, as I suspect, George and Rosamund were both involved in the Craft, then it is more than likely that he would have passed on any of Rosamund's artifacts, her magical tools, her herb cabinet and books, to someone in the Craft who would appreciate them. Edith is the obvious choice, as she is the only one we know of who remained in contact with Gerald Gardner and was living in the same road.

34. An early display at the Museum of Magic and Witchcraft entitled "Tools etc. belonging to a noted Witch who died in 1953"

Now, by the time Gardner was writing to Cecil Williamson about Rosamund's cabinet of drawers, both Gerald and Cecil had been co-operating in the running of the Museum of Magic and Witchcraft on the Isle of Man. Gerald took over the running of the museum in 1954 and, to start with, the captions to the exhibits looked rather amateurish. I think Illustration 34 opposite shows this clearly. It appears to show a set of drawers, which might well be Rosamund's, together with weighing scales, a pestle and mortar and other paraphernalia used for herb preparation.

The caption, which appears to have been partly typed and partly written, not very skilfully, with a guided drawing stencil, reads:

> TOOLS ETC BELONGING TO A NOTED WITCH WHO
> DIED IN 1953
>
> This is a very good example of things used by the Village Herbalist type of Witch. These things are deposited by some of her relations who do not want their name to be known.

The caption seems to have changed by 1959, when the American writer, Daniel Mannix, visited the museum. He noted the caption as saying:

> As a tribute to Aunt Agatha, one of our most outstanding witches, this collection of paraphernalia which she used is affectionately dedicated. Presented by her family in loving memory, 1951.[2]

Well-respected witch and author, Patricia Crowther, who was initiated by Gardner in 1960, mentioned to me that, when she first met him, he used to refer rather mysteriously to "Aunt Agatha". It may be that, on searching round for a pseudonym, Gardner picked on the character of "Aunt Agatha", who appears in P.G. Wodehouse's *The Inimitable Jeeves*[3], a formidable figure with which Gardner was doubtless familiar.

---

[2]   Daniel P. Mannix Witchcraft's Inner Sanctum *True Magazine* (August 1959) p 78.
[3]   P. G. Wodehouse *The Inimitable Jeeves* (Herbert Jenkins 1923).

By 1958, a guidebook to the museum had been published[4]. It seems likely that this was written by Doreen Valiente some time before her split with Gerald Gardner in 1957. The section relating to these items reads in part as follows:

> *Case No. 1. A large number of objects belonging to a witch who died in 1951, lent by her relatives who wish to remain anonymous. These are mostly things which had been used in the family for generations. Most of them are for making herbal cures.*

And also:

> *Case No. 5. A collection of objects used by witches, lent by an existing coven of witches. Naturally, they have only lent articles which they are not using, hence the collection consists chiefly of implements for the making of herbal cures and charms; there is, however, one very fine ritual wand, and a curious old desk containing seven secret drawers, in which they used to hide some of their possessions.*

This appears to be the case illustrated in a photograph appearing in Doreen Valiente's *The Rebirth of Witchcraft*.[5] Patricia Crowther gives a more detailed description of one of the items in this photograph:

> *One case in the museum was of great interest to me. Among other items it contained a large wooden box with a mirror inside the lid and paintings of the God and Goddess on either side. It held a miscellany of vials, charms, talismans and knives, and the latter had curious signs incised on them.*[6]

It is quite clear that this description is of the box illustrated in Doreen Valiente's book rather than the chest of drawers in the earlier photograph.

---

[4] G. B. Gardner *The Story of the Famous Witches Mill at Castletown, Isle of Man* (The Photochrom Co Ltd., 1958).

[5] Doreen Valiente *The Rebirth of Witchcraft* (Hale, 1989).

[6] Patricia Crowther *One Witch's World* (Hale, 1998) p 27.

However, it is clear that one, if not both, of these chests did originate with Rosamund Sabine, as did the edition of Culpeper which is in Gerald Gardner's library.

35. The display case in the Museum of Magic and Witchcraft housing items lent by the Southern Coven of British Witches

All this enables us to be reasonably sure that Rosamund was interested in and knowledgeable about the collection, preservation and use of herbs in ways both medicinal and magical.

13
Dorothy - One of the Old Sort

Prologue

This probably didn't happen, but it might have ...

Scene: Bethersden, near Ashford, Kent

It was a fine day in early spring 1949 and the village street in Bethersden was already busy with activity. This activity centred on the larger of the two village shops, Boorman's, directly opposite the village pub, The George.

And less than a hundred yards away was a gate which marked the entrance to the village churchyard, where a path of the local fossiliferous limestone known as Bethersden Marble started its route past the church and through the hopfields to the large mass of Lamberden Woods.

Between the church and Boorman's stood two cottages, out of one of which a lady and a gentleman emerged through the open front door. Behind them in the hallway was what looked like a sedan chair, which reputedly housed a telephone.

Walking down the garden path and out of the front gate, they made for the shop. The gentleman was Arthur Stuart Beazley, a stockbroker, who seemed to be known and liked by everyone in the village. With him, of a somewhat stout appearance and reddish face, and wearing what looked like a very expensive pearl necklace, was Dorothy St. Quintin Fordham, a rich widow from Highcliffe in Hampshire, who was staying with him for a few days, for he was more than just her stockbroker: he had become her friend.

As they approached the shop, a short friendly-looking woman in her late fifties was coming out of the door with her groceries in a string bag. She was also pushing a three-year-old boy in his push-chair and about to cross the road.

"Good morning, Mrs. Jennings" Beazley smiled. "I've been thinking about your daughter's problem with finding somewhere for her Cub pack to meet. Mrs. Fordham reminded me that she let her local Guide company meet in the Friar's Rest in the grounds of her house, and I'm wondering whether the room above my garage might be suitable. Perhaps you could ask Ruby to come and have a look at it. Oh, by the way, I should have introduced you. This is Mrs. Dorothy Fordham, who's staying with me for a few days. And this is Mrs. Lottie Jennings, a stalwart in the village."

It was then Dorothy's turn to speak: "Pleased to meet you, Mrs. Jennings. And who is this little chap with those marvellous golden curls?"

"Oh, this is my grandson, down from London for a few days with his parents. This is Philip ... Philip Heselton."

'Old Dorothy' is the only person other than Dafo whom Gerald Gardner mentions by name in association with the witch cult. Indeed, it was Doreen Valiente's investigations, published as 'The Search for Old Dorothy'[1] which inspired my own research activities, some results of which appear in the pages of this book. So, I have decided to include a chapter on Dorothy at this point because of that, although I am now clear that her influence on the development of the witch cult was indirect at best.

Despite the revelations which these investigations unearthed, Dorothy remains an enigmatic figure. For some, her role as High Priestess of the New Forest Coven was self-evident and unchal-

---

[1]   Janet and Stewart Farrar *The Witches' Way* (Hale, 1984) Appendix A pp. 283-293.

lengeable. Others were equally certain that she was not involved in witchcraft in any way.

In my attempts to resolve these apparently unreconcilable opinions, I was fortunate in being introduced to two people who knew Dorothy well and was therefore able to gain more insight into her personality than I had obtained from written sources. Through talking with them I have obtained a vivid impression of her character and personality and about some, at least, of the features of her life.

As I have already mentioned, it was Doreen Valiente's 'Search for Old Dorothy' which inspired my own researches, and it was Doreen who provided the first details of Dorothy's early life.

I go in some detail into Dorothy's ancestry in my book *Wiccan Roots*[2], but for the present purposes we will start with Dorothy's birth on 19th January 1880 at Umbala in India. Her father, Thomas St. Quintin Clutterbuck (1839-1910), was a Captain in the 14th Sikhs. Her mother was Ellen Anne Clutterbuck (née Morgan) (1857-1920).

Thomas retired from the Indian Army in January 1889, the year in which he attained the age of 50. By 1891, Thomas, Ellen and Dorothy were living, with two servants, in Merrifield House in Cornwall, just across the water from the Devonport Dockyards, Plymouth. Ten years later, in 1901, the family were at Oldford House, Selwood, near Frome, Somerset.

These glimpses of the family every 10 years from the census suggests that they did not settle in any one place for very long, a trait which seems to be quite common amongst those who could afford it. However, various sources, including her commonplace books, suggest that Dorothy was particularly familiar with the middle stretches of the Thames valley in Oxfordshire, in particular Henley and Whitchurch, together with Ditchley, also in Oxfordshire.

---

[2] Philip Heselton (2000) pp. 126-138.

In 1908, when Thomas was 70 years old and living at Gilpin's Cottage, Boldre, on the edge of the New Forest, he spotted Chewton Mill House, which had closed as a working watermill and was on offer to lease from the Hon. Edward James Montagu Stuart Wortley of the Highcliffe Castle estate.

The Mill House is situated in the steep-sided and wooded Chewton Glen which carries the Walkford Brook, which rises at the southern edge of the New Forest, down to the sea near Highcliffe. It is the first building you come across in the glen itself on walking up the footpath alongside Walkford Brook from the sea shore. The significance of this spot as a landing place has long been recognised, as Olive Samuel points out:

> *When England was apprehensive of invasion by the Spanish Armada in 1588, Chewton was defended by 200 men ... as opposed to Christchurch being allotted only 165 men for its defence. Chewton was considered a more likely landing place than Christchurch.*[3]

In later years the wooded nature of Chewton Glen plus the presence of quicksands at the mouth of the Walkford Brook made it an attractive smuggling route on dark nights (and they would be very dark in the days before street lights) for those who knew the 'lie of the land'.

It was clear to Thomas and Ellen that certain alterations and building works to the Mill House were going to be necessary before they would have a house which would be to their requirements and expectations of comfort.

Ironically, the first rent payment fell due the month of Thomas' death, in September 1910. Whilst a relative newcomer to the village, Thomas took an active interest in village events and was associated with the Highcliffe Stuart-Wortley Scouts, probably one of the first Boy Scout troops in the country, since the first

---

[3] Olive J. Samuel *Chewton Bunny, Highcliffe - The History of a Romantic Glen* (Olive J. Samuel, 1986) p. 2.

scout camp had taken place only three years previously, on Brownsea Island in nearby Poole Harbour.

36. The Mill House, Highcliffe: Dorothy's home
from the 1920s until she died in 1951

Dorothy's mother continued to live at the Mill House for another ten years until her own death in 1920. She had a gift for poetry and passed on to Dorothy not only her own volume of verses but also the ability to write in a similar vein. Her verses are full of love for and awareness of nature.

The late Gurth Brooke was born in 1920 and I was privileged to talk with him when he was in his nineties. He knew both Gerald Gardner and Dorothy well and gave me many insights into their characters. I quote from that talk and also from the interviews he gave to local historian, Ian Stevenson:

> *If a great novelist like, we'll say, Thomas Hardy, was to have written Dorothy's biography, I think the critics would have said "Look, you couldn't have a character like this. It's too fantastical altogether". But that was what she was. She was a quite remarkable character.*[4]

---

4   Interview Gurth Brooke and Ian Stevenson 19 November 2004.

He said about her that she had: ... *all the best qualities of Queen Elizabeth Tudor and all the worst qualities of Mary Queen of Scots.*[5]

She also had a quality which she shared with Gerald Gardner: to tell the literal truth whilst giving a misleading impression. Gurth gives an example of this:

> *Dorothy was very reluctant to give a direct negative answer if it wasn't to her advantage. If, let us suppose, that she had never been to Paris, and you said to her "Have you seen the Mona Lisa in the Louvre?" she wouldn't say no, she would say "Oh, well. Who hasn't?", giving the impression that she had been there. And I think if she had been talking to Gardner and Gardner had asked her if she was interested in witchcraft, she wouldn't have said no. She would have said "Well, I suppose lots of people have some slight fascination for the subject". She wouldn't have known anything about it herself, but she wouldn't have given the impression she knew nothing about it. She had that way of giving an oblique answer which ... worked to her special benefit.*[6]

Gurth said she was "completely self-willed and would get her way regardless of the consequences". He called her "a formidable personality". "She could be intensely kind and generous but if anyone got on the wrong side of her, it would be "off with his head!" No compunction about it at all."

One example of this seems to be the case of Charles Edward Byron Du Cane (1910-1996). He was in the R.A.F. during the war and it is obvious from Dorothy's diaries that she had got to know him very well indeed before he was sent abroad to India. In her will dated July 1949, she left him £5000, plus paintings, silver and her cars. In a codicil dated January 1950 she revokes this completely. The reason for this action is not known. He obviously displeased Dorothy in quite a serious way. One can only speculate.

---

5   Interview Gurth Brooke and Ian Stevenson 22 September 2009.
6   Interview Gurth Brooke and Ian Stevenson 19 November 2004.

There is a post-script to this. When Dorothy's commonplace books were on display in Bournemouth in 1986, following their discovery on a solicitor's shelves and there was some publicity in the local paper, those who were exhibiting them received a telephone call from a Mr. Du Cane, who said that they were "as green as grass about Mrs. Fordham" and that the best thing they could do with the commonplace books was to burn them.[7]

Gurth concluded:

> *She was the sort of person one doesn't see nowadays - the great eccentrics, of which this district had quite a few. She was probably the greatest of the lot.*

Prior to the Great War, Dorothy was living with Elizabeth Slatter in Whitchurch, Oxfordshire, where Elizabeth's father, Rev. John Slatter, MA, was Rector as well as being an honorary Canon of Christ Church, Oxford.

In September 1914, Dorothy was living at Mill House, Highcliffe and became a Voluntary Aid Detachment (V.A.D.) nurse, in the Brockenhurst British War Hospital. Brockenhurst, a village or small town in the heart of the New Forest, was officially designated as a key hospital centre by the War Office. Its proximity to the major port of Southampton and its position on a railway line made it an ideal location for receiving injured troops shipped back from France. A large temporary military hospital, popularly known as 'Tin Town', was constructed and other major buildings such as hotels were requisitioned as auxiliary hospitals.

In November 1915, Dorothy worked at the St. John's Ambulance Brigade Hospital, 2 Bodorgan Road, Bournemouth. In April 1916 she transferred to the Officers' Hospital, Highcliffe. This was a convalescent home for wounded officers under the direction of Lady Carter, at Chewton Lodge, Highcliffe. It was while she was here that she became friendly with Elsie Brooke, Gurth's mother.

---

7   Philip Heselton (2000) Chapter 11.

Dorothy spent the remainder of the war working at the Hants 122 Hospital. I suspect that it was during these war duties that Dorothy learned to drive.

How well she had learned to drive might be a point for contemplation, however, for, in 1927, Dorothy was involved in a road accident. In June of that year, she was driving her car, with her companion, Elizabeth Slatter, as passenger, en route from Highcliffe to Exeter, and was approaching the Toller Down cross-roads at Corscombe, Dorset, from the Maiden Newton direction, when she hit a cyclist, a Miss Edith Smith, a domestic servant of Bridport, Dorset.

Apparently, Dorothy was driving slowly, looking for a shady place to have lunch. The cyclist's companion warned her that a car was coming but she failed to stop and carried on across the cross-roads. Dorothy's car hit her, and she died that same evening from the injuries sustained.

At the inquest, Dorothy said that she had driven a car for the previous five years in every county in England except Essex and Suffolk and extensively in France and Italy. She had never previously had an accident.

A verdict of accidental death was returned.[8]

Dorothy was not always the wealthy woman that she later became. She was adept at needlework, making tablecloths and quilts for pin money. The embroidered cover of one of her commonplace books is probably her own work.

After the war, Dorothy and her mother were saved financially by the aforementioned Elizabeth Slatter. She was 27 years older than Dorothy and they probably got to know each other initially via the Anglican Church, for Dorothy's great uncle, Rev. James C Clutterbuck, was Vicar at Long Wittenham, in Berkshire, on the banks of the River Thames just eight miles south of Oxford.

---

[8]   *Western Gazette* 26 June 1927.

Elizabeth was a contemporary of Alice Liddell, made famous by Lewis Carroll (Charles Lutwidge Dodgson) in *Alice's Adventures in Wonderland*, published in 1865. She was one of the young girls whom Dodgson liked to photograph, and there are two photographs of her with the titles of 'Bessie Slatter' and 'Bessie Slat[t]er and pet guinea pig'.

Elizabeth came to live at the Mill House, initially as Dorothy's mother's companion and, following the latter's death in 1920, as Dorothy's. I am informed that Elizabeth was reasonably well off, and the injection of her money enabled Dorothy to travel quite a bit. Indeed, it was probably in the winter of 1930-31 that Dorothy first met Rupert Oswald Fordham on a trip to the south of France. It is interesting, however, that Dorothy's great-grandfather, Robert Clutterbuck, lived for many years at Hinxworth Place, in the neighbouring village to Ashwell, Hertfordshire, ancestral home of the Fordhams. The Rev. Arthur Clutterbuck, Dorothy's uncle, was also vicar of Hinxworth from 1886 to 1907. I suspect that down the years there were local contacts between their families, which Gerald Gardner has characterised as 'county'.

Known to Dorothy as Oswald, Rupert Oswald Fordham was born on 23rd March 1861, and was therefore some 19 years older than her. He was heir to the family firm of Fordham's Ashwell Brewery.

The Fordhams were a noted family, having estates at Odsey and Ashwell on the border of Hertfordshire and Cambridgeshire. They had been brewers in Ashwell since the early 1800s. Oswald's father, Edward King Fordham (1810-1889) was a prominent landowner and a Justice of the Peace for the counties of Hertford, Cambridge and Bedford and was Deputy Lieutenant for Bedfordshire, and High Sheriff in 1884.

Edward, together with Oswald's uncle Herbert, owned the family brewery business, which was a thriving one. Albert Sheldrick writes that:

*the pleasant aroma of malt still drifted over the village and
lorry loads of Fordham's ales went out to quench the thirst
of folks in at least four counties until World War Two ...[9]*

Rupert Oswald Fordham, who, along with his brother, Wolverley, was educated at Rugby School, is described as a "brewery pupil". He obviously had a share in the business and is always later described as being "of independent means". Like his father, he became a Justice of the Peace.

However, Oswald had had an unfortunate marital life, in that his first two wives had died, each after seven years of marriage and his third wife, Blanche, had become mentally ill and was living in a nursing home.

In 1893, Oswald married Caroline O'Malley, widow of Sir William O'Malley, and in June 1894 he acquired Broom Hall, a stately home and grounds near Biggleswade in Bedfordshire, only a few miles from Ashwell. Caroline died of cancer in 1900, at the age of 38, leaving almost £30,000 in her will.

Oswald married again in 1905. This was to Janet Elizabeth, daughter of William Durning Holt, of Liverpool. The Durning Holts were a prominent Liverpool family, involved in Liberal politics. Janet died from a diabetic coma in 1913, aged 45, leaving over £40,000 in her will.

Oswald married his third wife, Julia Blanche, in 1916. She was the daughter of Colonel George William Cox of the Indian Army. In about 1930 she became mentally ill and was cared for, at home and in a nursing home at Hayes, in Middlesex, for the rest of her life. She died in 1955.

In her commonplace book for 1942, Dorothy included two verses. One was dated August 1931 and was entitled "The Cornfields of Ashwell":

---

9   Albert A. Sheldrick *A Different World: Ashwell before 1939* (Cortney, n.d.) p 16

A Song before Sunrise - A Day at the Dawn
The dew on the Meadows - The Light on the Corn
Golden Cornfields, near Ashwell
For ever will be
Beloved, For your sake
Like Heaven to me.

Another one, with the same title and written the same month, goes as follows:

The golden Fields of Ashwell
Which set our Hearts a'dancing
Those Waves on Waves of rippling Corn.
Ah! Memories entrancing.
The Harvest Moon of August.
The Golden glowing weather
A Paradise for two, it was
For We, walked there together.

I think it is quite clear from this that, certainly at this stage in their relationship, Dorothy seemed to be very much in love with Oswald. I suspect that they must have fallen in love and decided to live together. Dorothy was obviously the more determined because by April 1931 she had had a self-contained extension to Mill House approved, and I am guessing that this was intended to provide some independent accommodation for Oswald. He moved in to Mill House by Autumn 1931 or Spring 1932 because he appears on the 1932 Electoral Register as living there. In any case, his Broom Hall estate in Bedfordshire was put up for sale by auction in September 1932. Also, on 1st February 1935, Dorothy's mortgage on Mill House was paid off, presumably by Oswald.

At the beginning of November 1932, Oswald Fordham wrote a letter to the local paper on the down-to-earth subject of drainage.[10] However, a fortnight later, the paper reports that:

We regret to record the serious illness of Mr. Oswald
Fordham, of the Mill House, Highcliffe. A few days since

---

[10] *Christchurch Times* 5 November 1932.

Mr. Fordham had the misfortune to sustain a fall in the house, which at the time was considered painful but of no further concern. It has since transpired that Mr. Fordham as a consequence of this accident now lies in a precarious condition.[11]

I suspect that this accident did indeed have a profound effect on Oswald's health, for Gurth Brooke, for as long as he could remember, described Oswald:

Well, he was gaga ... he was an unattractive old man ... He wasn't really mentally aware and he became more and more mentally gaga as time went on ... There was nothing lovable about him. He was almost like a dummy. Most of the time he had a sort of nurse to look after him. He was physically very crippled and mentally not fully with it.

She was a very strong personality and she could manipulate people. And it is questionable how much old Fordham knew about what was going on. He certainly didn't know about all of it. He was just being carried along by her and dominated by her ... I don't think that he had any feelings at all. I think it was just that she sort of took control of him and trundled him along. His mental state was increasingly such that he didn't really know what was going on and didn't really mind. He was being looked after in comfortable circumstances, and that was it.[12]

However, Oswald was clearly well enough to engage in a substantial purchase in 1933. Whilst the living accommodation at Mill House was quite adequate, Oswald was clearly used to living in more comfort and space, and he was looking around the neighbourhood for something more suitable for a gentleman in his position. In 1933, he found what he was looking for. A large house in Station Road (now Hinton Wood Avenue) known as Latimers was for sale. Oswald bought it at the auction which took place in December 1933.

---

11 *Christchurch Times* 19 November 1932
12 Interview Gurth Brooke and Ian Stevenson 19 November 2004.

The house itself was not over-large, but it had three impressive southward-facing gables looking over the ornamental garden. From the look of the photograph accompanying the sales document and subsequent photographs, it would appear that fake half-timbering was added to the whole of the south elevation of the house after the purchase, making a striking alteration in its appearance, to say the least! The grounds were over four acres in extent and included a lawn, ornamental pond, kitchen garden, paddock and two cottages.

37. Croquet on the front lawn at Latimers.
Dorothy is second from the right and Oswald is second from the left

Even if Dorothy had wanted to marry Oswald for his money, she was not able to do so because Blanche Fordham was still alive and it is illegal under English law to be married to more than one person.

Divorce was difficult in the 1930s and severe mental illness of one partner was not yet acceptable as grounds for divorce. There were moves to get the law changed, particularly by the writer A P Herbert (1890-1971), whose novel *Holy Deadlock*, published in 1934, highlighted some of the absurdities of the existing divorce law.

Change did not come until the passing into law of the Matrimonial Causes Act 1937, which allowed divorce after five years if one of the partners had severe mental illness. Interestingly, Herbert wrote a play entitled *The White Witch*, performed in 1926.

It was generally known in the village, certainly amongst Dorothy's acquaintances, that Oswald's wife, Blanche, who was severely mentally ill (or 'incurably insane' as they would have said at the time), was living in a nursing home in Hayes, Middlesex. A regular sum was sent for her upkeep and their chauffeur, Hudson, was said to have been sent regularly with fruit and vegetables for her, a round trip of over 200 miles.

However, this was still in the future in early 1935, so, after some deliberation, Dorothy decided to act. The first thing to do was to make it known that Blanche Fordham had died, even though she didn't actually die for another twenty years. So one Spring day in 1935, Dorothy phoned up a few close friends, including her confidante, Elsie Brooke, Gurth's mother. "My dear" she announced. "Blanche Fordham's dead."

"Well", replied Mrs Brooke, "I suppose it's a blessed release".

"We'll be going up for the funeral next week", Dorothy remarked.

On the day set for the funeral, Dorothy surprised her chauffeur, Fred Hudson, by giving him the day off. "I'll drive us myself" she announced. He helped Dorothy and Oswald into the car, together with a large wreath.

Much later that day they returned and left the car in the charge of Hudson. He had been suspicious. It had been most unusual for Dorothy to want to drive the car herself. This reluctance possibly dated back to the incident in 1927 which I mentioned earlier. Anyway, Hudson looked at the mileometer: the car had done precisely ten miles since the morning, whereas the journey up to Middlesex and back would be in excess of 200 miles.

He began to realise that they had never been to a funeral at all and had probably sunk the wreath in a convenient pond. This, he suddenly began to see, was because there was no funeral to go to. Blanche Fordham was still alive! But Hudson was a loyal employee. He kept his suspicions to himself, at least until after Dorothy's death.

Not long afterwards, Dorothy announced that she and Oswald were going to go to Guernsey to be married by one of Oswald's family who was a clergyman. Whether this ever took place I do not know. However, we do know that on 8th August 1935, Rupert Oswald Fordham and Dorothy Clutterbuck went through a marriage ceremony at the Kensington Registry Office in London. Interestingly, Dorothy, who was 55 at the time, put down her age on the marriage certificate as 42!

I do not know why they went through this ceremony which they must have known was legally invalid. It was certainly not to lead people into thinking that they were married, because it was carried out with little fuss and no publicity. There is no report or mention of it in the *Christchurch Times*, for example, which might be expected to report on the marriage of what were then prominent citizens. But it is certainly true that the *Christchurch Times*, which reported regularly on the activities of the Mill House Players, was referring to Dorothy as 'Miss Clutterbuck' up until early 1935. By 1936 she was being referred to as 'Mrs Fordham'. She is also thus referred to in the electoral registers compiled in that and subsequent years. There were results leading from this which would not surface for several years, as we shall see.

Anyway, soon after this, Oswald transferred to Dorothy about £100,000 worth of brewery securities, the equivalent of many millions of pounds in today's money. Dorothy thus became a very wealthy woman.

I think that, latterly in their relationship, it probably was true that Dorothy was mostly interested in Oswald's money. This is perhaps indicated by an entry in her commonplace book for 23rd March 1942, the anniversary of Oswald's birthday. One might expect some pious and thoughtful reflection on his life and what he meant to her. Instead, what we get is:

> I've got a sixpence, a jolly jolly sixpence
> A sixpence which will last me all my life.
> I've sixpence due to lend, and sixpence too to spend
> And sixpence left to send unto my wife!

Now that she could afford it, Dorothy became extremely generous and lavish in entertaining. Gurth Brooke told me that she wanted to *vie with the big people of the district - the 'county' folk - and prove to be their equal.* He thought that for so long she felt that she had been classed as 'poor gentlefolk' and looked down upon.

Despite Oswald's purchase of Latimers in 1933, it was to be another three years before he, Dorothy and the servants are indicated on the electoral register as living there. I think it likely that they kept both houses on and that it was only gradually that the centre of operations focused on Latimers.

If Fordham was 'gaga' at that time, then it must have been Dorothy who added half-timbering to the main façade of Latimers, converting it, according to Gurth, into a Cheshire mansion.

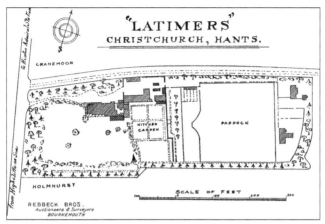

38. Plan of Latimers accompanying the 1933 sale documents

Dorothy was happy to have two houses - Mill House and Latimers - and made good use of both of them. She called them "The Fordham Houses" in her commonplace books. Gurth likened it to the summer and winter palaces of the Russian czars. Latimers was the summer palace and Mill House the winter palace. In winter, there were concerts and parties at Mill House and in the summer, garden parties, fêtes and croquet tournaments at Latimers.

Dorothy supported a whole range of organisations by holding garden parties at Latimers. These included the local Conservative Party, of which she was a very keen member; the Boy Scouts and Girl Guides; the Royal Victoria and West Hants Hospital; the Highcliffe and District Horticultural Society and the National Society for the Prevention of Cruelty to Children. There were also gymkhanas and tournaments of various sorts.

Dorothy could certainly afford to be extremely generous and lavish in her entertaining. It was, in part, that she wanted to be thought of as 'Lady of the Manor' and be accepted as part of the 'county' set.

Dorothy's reputation in the village was as someone who was known to be wealthy but who was generous with her money, whether it be hosting garden parties at Latimers, financing performances of the Mill House Players (of whom more later), or offering to finance the purchase of cliff-top land for public enjoyment.

39. A reception at the Mill House with Dorothy on the extreme left

It is rumoured that she used to stop her car outside a local shop and expected the shopkeeper to come out and take her order. Whether this was habitual or only an isolated occasion (perhaps she had broken her foot or something of that nature) I do not know. It may have been merely apocryphal as illustrating how her character was perceived in the village. Certainly in later years Maidie Doohan remembers Dorothy coming in regularly to Tugwell's chemist's shop where she worked.

Maidie was once invited into Mill House in rather unusual circumstances. It was during the war. She and her friend, June, were walking along the Glen:

> ... the gardener at Mill House was out and he called to us ... "Where are you going?" and we said we were going home along Montagu Road. ... So he said "No. You're not! Come in! You're not to be out". We could hear planes coming over. ... So he said "Come in the house. Don't stand outside. Mrs. Fordham isn't here at present: she's staying at

Latimers." And so we said "Oh!" And he said "Come in the house and I'll show you the house. And I was just gobsmacked! It's the most beautiful house inside. It had a minstrel's gallery and I remember the front door. It had about 40 brass door-knockers on it! All different shapes and sizes! I couldn't think why somebody would have so many different door-knockers! But he took us up and showed us round upstairs. Beautifully furnished. And in one room was a big double bed and on there there must have been a good twenty or thirty big picture hats of every colour and sort you could possibly wish to see. It just took my breath away. I'd never ever seen anything like that before in my life.[13]

After her mother's death in 1920, Dorothy took out the old mill wheel and converted the mill room so that it could be used as a rehearsal room for what would be a major interest of hers for the next 15 years or so - the Mill House Players. This room was known as the Music Room, and had a first floor gallery which, I imagine, would have been very useful for rehearsals. A statue stands on the outside wall above the window and has the inscription: 'Orpheus - Designed for this Music Room by RMD - Feb 1924'. The identity of 'RMD' is not known.

Gurth told me:

Dorothy put on the most lavish and expensive Gilbert and Sullivan performances at local halls, things like The Mikado and Iolanthe and The Yeomen of the Guard, all very thoroughly done with no expense spared at all. She would hire professionals from Bournemouth to sing the leading contralto, tenor and baritone parts and she always took the leading soprano part herself. Excruciating! When the top note was coming people were hanging onto the arms of their chairs. She used to get other people around the district to take the supporting parts and the lads and lasses in the village formed the chorus.

---

[13] Interview Maidie Doohan with Ian Stevenson 8 April 2005.

Reg Kitcher gives his memories of the period:

> ... *when I was 18 years old I was invited to join a group at Highcliffe in 1928 called the "Mill House Players". They were a bunch of local amateur singers and players both young and middle-aged from around the area and they intended to put on the Gilbert and Sullivan opera "The Mikado". We were all happy to meet down at the Mill House, Chewton Glen, to learn and rehearse every night of the week and on Sunday afternoons for about three months, previous to putting on the show for a week of evenings at Highcliffe and one night stands at Christchurch, Boscombe, Milford, New Milton, Brockenhurst and Lymington. We were conveyed to these halls by taxi and various private cars all arranged and financed by Miss Clutterbuck of the Mill House. We did one opera each year for about four years. It was through these shows that I met the girl who was to be my wife ...*[14]

As 1939 dawned, Oswald sustained further injuries which may well have hastened his death less than five months later. This was the result of a car crash on Friday 6th January:

> *At about four o'clock, when between Alton and Winchester, their chauffeur was following a heavy road lorry at a normal speed.*

> *Suddenly ahead, and so it is alleged, on the wrong side of the road, a saloon car, driven at an astonishing speed, collided with the lorry with great force. The saloon car was hurled up by the force of the impact and fell heavily upon the car behind, crushing the bonnet and engine.*

> *Mr. Fordham, who was seated beside the driver, had his legs thrust through into the engine, and the pipe he was smoking was smashed, leaving the stem still in his lips. Both he and the driver were pinioned by debris and had to be liberated. Mrs. Fordham, travelling behind, sustained*

---

[14] Reg Kitcher *My Early Years at Hinton Admiral and Highcliffe, Hampshire* (1910-1939) (Olive J. Samuel, 1985) pp 8-9.

only a twisted ankle, but their condition was such that four hours elapsed before they left for Highcliffe.

The road was strewn with wreckage of the two cars and the lorry, the drivers of which had to receive medical attention.

Alarming as this road smash must have been, yet Mr. and Mrs. Fordham and their chauffeur congratulate themselves upon a most narrow escape from tragic disaster.

Both Mr. and Mrs. Fordham are compelled to receive medical attention, and are confined to the house and, of course, the projected theatrical entertainment, which was in process of production, under the direction of Mrs. Fordham, is postponed until the week following Easter next.[15]

Whilst not the direct cause, this accident may have contributed to the death of Rupert Oswald Fordham on 31st May 1939 at the Mill House aged 78. The cause of death is given as hypostatic pneumonia and degenerative myocarditis.

In August 1939, following Oswald's death, Dorothy covenanted to "provide for the maintenance and comfort of Mrs. Blanche Fordham" after her death and she started to send monthly cheques for Mrs. Fordham's maintenance.

Oswald died intestate (i.e. without making a will) but Dorothy, claiming to be his widow, was granted Letters of Administration on 11th October 1939 in the sum of £613 7s 2d. These were challenged by Oswald's son by his first marriage, Rupert Granville Fordham. The challenge was upheld in the courts and an Order was made in the Probate Courts on 13th January 1941 revoking the Letters of Administration which had been granted in 1939 to Dorothy, and granting them to Rupert Granville Fordham, Oswald's only son. Costs were awarded against Dorothy.

Later that same year, and presumably as a direct result of this case, Dorothy changed her name by Deed Poll. On 7th November 1941,

---

[15] *Christchurch Times* 14 January 1939

she "... did thereby absolutely renounce and abandon the use of her surname of Clutterbuck and in lieu thereof assumed as from the date thereof the surname of St. Quintin-Fordham".

After the court judgement, everything came out into the open and Dorothy lost quite a few friends. She told Gurth's mother: "Elsie, it was sheer hell, but if I'd had my life over again I'd do just the same thing."

One result of the publicity[16] surrounding the court case was that the vicar of Highcliffe, Charles Gould, refused to give Dorothy communion. It was the only time that Gurth had known that happen in the Anglican church:

> *Well, Dorothy was not going to take that lying down and demanded an audience with the Bishop of Winchester, who was Dr. Cyril Garbett (1875-1955), who later became Archbishop of York. Dorothy didn't get the better of him, but apparently Garbett was impressed with this formidable figure that came before him to put her case.*

Whilst Gould was at Highcliffe, Dorothy used to attend the Priory Church in Christchurch. In 1943 Gould retired and Henry Brownlow took his place. He seemed to be more flexible in his approach and Dorothy was again allowed to take communion. After the war, attitudes seemed to change and people were quite prepared to be on good terms with her.

Gurth told Ian Stevenson that:

> *After her marriage affair blew up she did tend to have a little circle of rather questionable hangers-on, not genuine friends, people mostly younger than herself, that went there and picked up what they could, seeing that she was very generous ... Now they were quite separate from local people who were Dorothy's personal friends.[17]*

---

[16] *Daily Herald* 14 January 1941.
[17] Interviews Gurth Brooke and Ian Stevenson 19 November 2004 and 6 April 2005.

Now, I have no evidence for this, but it is possible, to say no more, that these may have been members of the wica.

Dorothy was one of countless "women of leisure" who kept commonplace books for the years 1942 and 1943. In Dorothy's case these were daily verses on a variety of topics, illustrated by the watercolours of Christine Wells, a local teacher and member of the Royal Watercolour Society. Whether there were others, I do not know, but these are the only ones that appear to have survived.

I gave a full account of these books in my *Wiccan Roots*[18] so all I will recount here are the main themes addressed by Dorothy's verses, and what they reveal about her character and possible link with the witch cult.

First of all, there are what I imagine to be typical of most commonplace books: entries relating to the cycle of the year, including birthdays and other anniversaries, and places that she had visited.

They show a rather different side to Dorothy than her outward personality would suggest; a more thoughtful side, one aware of and in tune with nature. Undoubtedly patriotic and outwardly conventional, they had verses on supporting the war effort and wartime hardships. But Dorothy also writes freely about fairies and nature spirits. Whether she actually believed in them I do not know, but it is, I think, significant that Dorothy quotes from her mother's Book of Verses, written at the Mill, which shows a similar awareness of the spirit behind nature. It is clear that Dorothy was carrying on a family tradition.

And in Dorothy's best friend, Katherine Oldmeadow, whose life and work I will be looking at in Chapters 15 and 16, we have a very good writer who not only believed in fairies and nature spirits but who included that belief in many of her stories, including those set in the very glen in which they both lived.

---

[18] Philip Heselton (2000) pp 156-176.

Dorothy was strongly aware of birds, animals and flowers, in her garden and in the wider context, including the trees of the New Forest, particularly May blossom. Indeed, in the pages of Dorothy's bible, which was found recently in the attic at Mill House, probably given to her as a confirmation gift, there are quite a few pressed flowers which had been preserved.

Roses have for many years been a popular flower, but Dorothy was obsessed with them, a trait she shared with many of the other characters we come across in the pages of this book.

14
The Protectress

I was reading a passage in Gerald Gardner's *Witchcraft Today* when I began to understand Dorothy's possible role in the whole thing. With his friends, the wica, he is discussing "the Devil", a term which he says they never use, but knew what he meant. Margaret Murray, whose *The Witch Cult in Western Europe*[1] was published in 1921, wrote about the Devil as being an office-holder in each coven. Gerald seemed to be familiar with this and probably asked the witches who was the Devil in their coven. A high priestess said to him:

> *"I wish one of the old sort, a great protector, would turn up, who had a great big house and grounds to lend us for meetings. If he really were of us, I wouldn't bother too much about his vast learning; I'd appoint him and teach him the job."*[2]

It seems clear that Dorothy performed that role while she was alive. There is some evidence in her commonplace books, which were for 1942 and 1943, that she had had some teaching from the wica, but had not fully understood it.

This was the period after Gould had refused to give her communion but before Brownlow had taken over. Whilst in no way did this seem to affect her commitment to the Anglican Church, it may have made her more sympathetic to the beliefs and practices of the wica, as, by this time, Dorothy would, I suspect, have a reasonably good idea of what was going on.

---

[1] Margaret Alice Murray *The Witch-Cult in Western Europe: A Study in Anthropology* (Oxford, 1921).

[2] Gardner (1954) pp. 131-132.

Now, Dorothy died on 12th January 1951. If the wica had been meeting in her house or grounds, even on occasions, this arrangement would presumably cease on her death. *Witchcraft Today* was published in 1954. It therefore seems likely that Gardner's discussion with the high priestess quoted above, would probably have been in 1953, just enough time for the witches to "make do" with other premises whilst remembering the "good old days" when Dorothy's houses and gardens were available. As Gerald Gardner says: *Witchcraft today is largely a case of "make do"*.[3]

It must be asked, however, how much Dorothy knew about what was going on. In other words, did she know that witches were conducting rituals on her property and, if so, did she mind?

I certainly know of one village hall which is occasionally hired for rituals by a coven, and I am told that the village hall committee are entirely ignorant of what goes on there, but they trust the individuals making the booking.

At least initially, I think the same applied with Dorothy. She would have been approached by someone who knew her, like George Sabine or Katherine Oldmeadow, and, because she trusted them, she allowed her 'spare house' to be used.

But, which was her spare house? Gurth Brooke referred to the 'summer and winter palaces' of Latimers and Mill House respectively, but where were Dorothy and the servants 'a few days after the war began', which is when Gerald says his initiation took place?

The month of September 1939 was highly significant in more ways than one. It was, of course, on the 3rd of that month that Britain declared war on Germany following that country's invasion of Poland. It was also the month in which Gerald Gardner, the first and greatest publicist of modern pagan witchcraft, was initiated into what he called 'the witch cult'.

---

3   Gardner (1954) p 125.

A third event occurred that month, largely as a result of the former and which throws considerable new light on the latter.

The National Registration Act would provide for a register to be compiled which would have details of individuals' names, addresses, sex, marital status, date of birth and occupation. The Registrar General, who had the splendid name of Sir Sylvanus Percival Vivian, announced that National Registration Day would be on Friday 29th September 1939. On that date, a register was taken of the 40 million inhabitants of England and Wales for the purpose of issuing identity cards, the administration of rationing and doubtless for other reasons. Forms were issued to every household and 65,000 enumerators were employed to collect the completed forms and to issue identity cards. With some exceptions, this information has been available online since 2015, and very revealing it is too!

To start with, it made me think very deeply about where it was that Gerald Gardner was initiated.

Doreen Valiente, in the appendix, 'The Search for Old Dorothy' in Janet and Stewart Farrar's *The Witches' Way*[4] concluded that it was in The Mill House, Highcliffe-on-Sea and, after looking at the evidence, I agreed with her.

Bracelin[5] states that the house in which Gerald was initiated "belonged to Old Dorothy". One interesting thing about that account, however, is something else. It has been stated numerous times that Gardner was initiated by Dorothy Clutterbuck ("Old Dorothy"). Nowhere in Gerald's books does it say so. It merely says that he was initiated. Indeed, the wording used suggests strongly to me that Dorothy wasn't actually present. Note that Bracelin[6] says the house "belonged to" Old Dorothy. If she was actually there, living in the house, one would be unlikely to use that phrase. You'd probably just say something like "He was taken to

4   Janet and Stewart Farrar *The Witches' Way* (Hale 1984) pp. 283-293.
5   Bracelin p 165.
6   ibid.

meet Dorothy Clutterbuck. Her house was a big one ..." However, if the owner were not present, the phrase "belonged to" might well be applied. Also, the phrase "she invariably wore ..." suggests to me hearsay - what Gardner had been told rather than direct experience of her.

Whilst one might refer familiarly to someone as "Old so-and-so", one wouldn't be introduced to them in that way. "Old Dorothy" is just the sort of epithet that one applies to someone who is not actually there. If Dorothy had been present, the book would have said something like: "He met a lady called Dorothy Clutterbuck ..." and would then proceed to give Gardner's impressions of her. It seems clear to me that his friends were talking about someone who was known to them but a little bit distant - not one of their regular companions.

Now, Dorothy did have two residences in Highcliffe. As well as Mill House, she also owned Latimers, off Station Road. As I have already mentioned, Latimers was Oswald Fordham's house, whereas Dorothy preferred Mill House. They compromised, living part of the year in one and part of the year in the other, the so-called summer and winter palaces. This regular move, of course, also involved all or most of the servants.

Following Oswald Fordham's death in May 1939, Dorothy, I think, felt somewhat freer to live where she wanted. Oswald died in Latimers and electoral registers and other sources suggest that Dorothy was there, with the servants, throughout the summer.

Let us suppose that Dorothy receives the form to fill in for the Register. She may have felt, possibly correctly, that one of her houses might be in danger of being requisitioned for military purposes or to accommodate children evacuated from the cities.

So, Dorothy and the servants all moved to Mill House in good time for the 29th, when the form had to be filled in. Indeed, in the Register we find that Dorothy and her servants are all at Mill House whereas Latimers is completely uninhabited. This ties in with something that Gurth told me, that in September 1939 Dorothy stood her ground and didn't evacuate to a safer part of the country, which she could well have afforded to do. She opened Latimers to the troops, and he felt that she was intensely patriotic and public spirited.

Bracelin says that Gardner was initiated "a few days after the war started"[7], in good time to be in the vacant Mill House before it was occupied. I'd like Mill House to be the place where Gerald was initiated because its design and setting and the whole 'feel' of the place are far more 'witchy' than Latimers. I think on the balance of probabilities it was, but, as I am about to describe, I may well be wrong!

To return to George Sabine, he may not have been in the Home Guard for very long, but on at least one occasion there was a direct link between him and Dorothy Fordham.

He put himself forward as P.R.I. in the Highcliffe Local Defence Volunteers, the forerunners of the Home Guard, of which Gerald Gardner was also a member. John Yeowell tells me that P.R.I. "stood for President of the Regimental Institute, which is not as grand as it sounds. When I was in the Army sixty-odd years ago the P.R.I. was chairman of the canteen committee."[8]

After Dorothy and Oswald acquired Latimers in 1933, they adapted a building in the grounds, which became known as the Friar's Rest and, later, as the Garden House. I think it was intended as an 'olde worlde' inn, as there is a freestanding hanging inn sign in the photograph.

---

[7] ibid. p 165.
[8] John Yeowell letter to the author 5 November 2002.

40. The only known photograph of the Friar's Rest

The inn sign also appears in the painting by Christine Wells, which illustrated the poem which Dorothy wrote about it in her commonplace book[9]:

> *Quaint little house in the garden alone*
> *Standing demurely there, all on your own.*
> *Black & white walls, & its Norfolk reed roof*
> *It's a fairy tale house, if you're telling the truth.*
> *A garden of lavender, Box bushes small*
> *And round it grey Egg cups to finish the wall.*
> *St. Francis takes care of its birds, as they roam*
> *And inside is all that you need for a Home.*
> *Tiny chintz curtains of soft primrose yellow*
> *Chairs of the same, & a floor red & mellow*
> *Lights, & a fire, & a table to dine*
> *Tea cups & silver - Decanters for wine*
> *Tea parties & meetings have been held at the Rest*
> *and also for war work its done its small best*
> *First, a canteen for soldiers by day*
> *Then for the men learning Radio-Ray.*
> *High up the Friar swings there on his sign*
> *Inviting his Patrons to tea & to dine.*

---

9   6 July 1942.

41. The Friar's Rest: Christine Wells' watercolour illustration
in Dorothy's commonplace book for July 1942

Whether George was instrumental in Dorothy's opening the Garden House to the troops, I do not know, but the *Christchurch Times* of 6 July 1940 reports as follows:

Mrs. Fordham provides Troops with Club. Comfort and homeliness make instant appeal. A pleasing yet informal little ceremony took place at Latimers, Highcliffe, on Friday last, when Mrs. Rupert Fordham very kindly instituted a club in original and entirely charming surroundings, called the Garden House, for the use of the military, now stationed in Highcliffe; the Garden House stands in the beautiful grounds of Latimers.

In the club the apartments have been furnished with those items calculated to make it of the maximum attraction to young men, with all the games from the inevitable darts to billiards. In addition to tea, light refreshments will be obtainable at a trifling cost. Literature and reading matter will be there in abundance, as well as a plentiful supply of writing paper, envelopes and postcards.

We have had the pleasure of being shown over the club and grounds by Mrs. Fordham herself. That it will provide a haven of peace and quietude for the men who are here literally defending our hearths and homes is a certainty, and that its comfort will appeal is equally certain.

The troops are very cordially invited to make use of the club at once, and to consider themselves members of what is for all intents and purposes a most excellent and homely club.

To all military men now in the district, we with confidence assure them of the cordial welcome which awaits them at the Garden Club. The hours at which it is open are from 5.30 to 7.45 p.m.[10]

George was certainly instrumental in getting the invitation extended to include the L.D.V. (Home Guard) as his letter, which is given prominence below the above report, makes clear:

I am directed by Headquarters, Local Defence Volunteers, Highcliffe, to ask you to be good enough, through the medium of the "Christchurch Times" to inform the members of the Local Defence Volunteers in Highcliffe, that Mrs. Rupert Fordham has very kindly consented to allow the volunteers of Highcliffe to consider themselves honorary members of the Garden House, which she has instituted at her residence, Latimers, for the use of the troops here.

The hours during which the club house will be open are from 5.30 p.m. until 7.45 p.m. Mrs. Fordham has also thrown open the gardens and lawns for the use and pleasure of the members.

I am also directed by Headquarters to express our sincere thanks for this patriotic gesture of Mrs. Fordham, and know it will be much appreciated by our members.[11]

Although the painting and photograph of the Friar's Rest do not show the building in any detail, to those who are at all familiar with the history of the Craft, it bears a striking resemblance to the 'witch's cottage' which Gerald Gardner acquired from J.S.M. Ward

---

[10] *Christchurch Times* 6 July 1940.

[11] ibid.

in 1945.[12] Certainly Dorothy's description of black and white walls and Norfolk reed roof fit the 'witch's cottage' exactly, i.e. half-timbered with a thatched roof.

Gardner, as a member of the Home Guard, would doubtless have been familiar with the Friar's Rest, both outside and inside. This may have been the reason why he wanted to acquire the 'witch's cottage': that it reminded him of the Friar's Rest. And perhaps this had such an impact on him because there is the intriguing possibility that the Friar's Rest might actually have been where he was initiated.

If I am wrong in my identification of the location of Gerald Gardner's initiation, and it was indeed at Latimers, I think a good case could be made for it being in the Friar's Rest rather than the main house. Dorothy was in the habit of letting it out to different groups in any case.

It sounds from the description in Dorothy's poem earlier in this chapter that the Friar's Rest was isolated from other habitations, having its own facilities, including an open fire, and in many ways ideal for ritual purposes. And, as I say earlier, it could have imprinted itself so strongly on Gerald's mind that he had no hesitation in acquiring the 'Witch's Cottage' from J.S.M. Ward in 1945.

So, Mill House or the Friar's Rest? At this stage, I really can't decide!

---

[12] Heselton (2003) pp 160-167.

15
Katherine Oldmeadow -
Writer of Faery and Forest

I am putting forward the idea that the witch cult was never really invented at any particular moment, nor was it, in my view, something which came through from the mists of antiquity, but rather something which evolved amongst a group of individuals who were living in Hampshire in the 1930s. And it continues to evolve.

For most of the individuals I have been researching for this book we have relatively little that they have written themselves. The one exception is Katherine Oldmeadow (1878-1963), who wrote over 23 books during the period from 1919 to 1958 and who, in those books, left a wealth of material to study, and very revealing it is.

She was the author of, mainly, girls' school stories, and I thought that it might be fruitful to look in some detail at the themes she introduced into her stories to see how they may have been incorporated into the witch cult as it evolved.

I wrote about Katherine Oldmeadow at greater length in my book *Gerald Gardner and the Cauldron of Inspiration*.[1] The concept of the cauldron is probably an appropriate one when considering the origin of what Gardner knew by the name of the witch cult. The individuals I have identified as being most likely to have been involved are those who had a variety of interests, in esoteric and other fields which, when brought together, would provide a fertile ground within which the witch cult could emerge.

---

[1]   Philip Heselton (2003) pp. 34-63.

Katherine Oldmeadow certainly had these interests in abundance. I first heard about her and her books from Ian Stevenson, the local historian in Highcliffe. He told me that she was a close friend of Dorothy Clutterbuck and lived only a quarter of a mile from her. It occurred to me that those books might be worth reading. I was right!

Katherine Louise Oldmeadow was born on 10th June 1878 in Chester. Her father was Deputy Chief Constable for the city. She was the youngest of nine children, three boys and six girls. She was not the only writer in the family, as one of her brothers was Ernest James Oldmeadow (1867-1949), who converted to Catholicism at the age of 30 and became editor of *The Tablet*, the Catholic newspaper, from 1923 to 1936. He wrote several adventure stories, including *The North Sea Bubble* about a German invasion of England.[2]

Some time after 1911, Katherine (known familiarly as Kit) and her sister, Anne (Nance), moved from Chester, where they grew up, to settle in Highcliffe. (Interestingly, I had an Auntie Kit and an Auntie Nance, who were really great-aunts.) Why they moved I do not yet know, although Nance was doing a bit of teaching.

42. A family picnic in the 1920s. Katherine Oldmeadow in the centre with wide-brimmed hat. The boy on the right is Gurth Brooke

[2] Ernest Oldmeadow *The North Sea Bubble* (Grant Richards, 1906).

However, shortly afterwards, their married sister, Edith, and her husband, Arthur Gavin Wallace Lawrie, whom she had married in 1898, returned from a life in India where he had been a civil engineer and photographer. They bought The Glen House, situated at the corner of Lymington Road and Mill Lane, only a few hundred yards from The Mill House, Dorothy's home and all moved in together.

Arthur Lawrie wrote and produced amateur dramatics. Dorothy also wrote in her commonplace book about him:

> ... he could also tell your Fate,
> if it were dull or bright.
> He only has to hold your hand,
> For he has second sight.[3]

Gurth Brooke, who knew Katherine well, told Ian Stevenson:

> They were a very united family. Mrs. Lawrie was by far the most practical, down-to-earth member of the family. Nance was quite intelligent but didn't possess the talent that Kit had for writing. But Kit was the quietest and most introverted of them.[4]

Gurth also spoke about Katherine and her approach to religion:

> ... in the first instance she was Church of England and then she converted to Roman Catholicism, but I think was never really very comfortable with it, and I think she lapsed or backed off for a time ... I don't know whether there was some pressure or incentive, but Kit was such a very individual character, with her own beliefs and outlooks, and perhaps she didn't find that Roman Catholicism was a very comfortable frame for her point of view. It didn't allow enough, shall we say, mental freedom. She definitely had her own ideas. ... she didn't bring religion into things at all.

---

3   entry for 28 March 1942.
4   Gurth Brooke interview with Ian Stevenson 19 November 2004.

*She was not one of the, as one would say, "churchy" people.
She wasn't like that at all.[5]*

Katherine was friendly with a variety of people of different backgrounds, as Ian Stevenson points out:

*Sipping tea from delicate china in Highcliffe Castle's
elegant Drawing Room might seem a world away from a
steaming brew in a tin mug beside a gypsy's shack just up
the road at Thorney Hill. Yet ... Katherine Oldmeadow
made many friends among the Thorney Hill gypsies and
took an interest in them and their customs. They were able
to help her with much information ...[6]*

It is clear that Dorothy held Katherine in high regard, so much so that she gave her and her family the commonplace books that she and Christine Wells had spent so many hours producing. There was certainly a strong bond of friendship between them, for Dorothy writes of her appreciation of Katherine being there in a time of need. She wrote in her commonplace book on what she believed was Katherine's birthday, 10th July 1942 (in fact, it was 10th June!):

*White roses bloomed & held their sway
When Katherine Oldmeadow came this way
And clever fairies round her cradle
Gave her a brilliant brain & able
Keen, dainty wit, a charming mind
And talents of outstanding kind
For, with her pen how many a page
She's made for folks of every age.
She's made them cry, & made them smile
With her inimitable style.
She bids you listen, bids you hark
To Ponies trotting in the dark
She says "My Darling, shut your eye.
The Gentlemen are going by."*

5   Gurth Brooke interview with Ian Stevenson 6 April 2005.
6   Ian Stevenson - Accompanying notes to the exhibition Costumes and Characters
    held at Highcliffe Castle 2001.

Here's to your Brilliance and your wit.
Here's to your health, my clever Kit.[7]

Conversely, Katherine is clearly writing about the Mill House when she says:

The figure of St. Francis, with a bird nestling on his shoulder, stands on an ancient mill stone, looking at the house whose hospitality is truly Franciscan; for all in trouble, poverty or sickness come knocking at the door and are received with open arms.[8]

The Mill House had such a figure.

Katherine lived at The Glen House for the rest of her life. She lost her sight in 1960, and died on 8th July 1963.

Katherine had some 23 books published between 1919 and 1958, in addition to her one non-fiction book entitled *The Folklore of Herbs*, published in 1946.

All of them reveal the sort of interests that would provide a sympathetic environment in which a witch cult might be expected to thrive.

Pre-eminently, there is a rich appreciation of Nature and of its experience evoking deep feelings in her characters. She was very much aware of and appears to have a very deep emotional response to the landscape around her, both Chewton Glen, which was close to her house, and the New Forest generally. For example:

Great deep glades, where the beech-leaves lay like a fairy carpet of magic colours, and scarlet and orange and yellow toadstools grew all ready to be spread for some elfin feast. The bracken was a baby forest of golden trees, and across

---

7   entry for 10 July 1942.
8   Katherine Oldmeadow *The Folklore of Herbs* (Cornish Bros., 1946) pp. 65-66.

the purple-brown, autumn-scented heather big spiders were spinning shining silver webs in the sunshine.[9]

It was the greatest fun getting ready for the night; though it really was not like night at all with a moon swinging like a great silver lantern over the Forest, and the only darkness lying in the shadows of the holly trees, which stood round the caravan like armed soldiers, their sober, prickly old heads crowned with yellow-tinted wreaths of honeysuckle.[10]

And the following is a very vivid description of what could be a ritual site in the heart of the New Forest, though I have not, so far, been able to identify it, and it is more probably the product of Katherine's very fertile imagination:

To see the Forest in all its fairy loveliness you must leave the king's highway and plunge boldly into the greenwood, or make friends with some tiny stream and let it lead you onward like a gay, singing comrade. It will show you the Forest's noblest trees, its most magical colours, and its rarest wild-flowers. Pandora and Rory knew this, and before they had gone many miles they left the forest road and plunged into a rough track through pine-woods. "We'll show you the King's Council Chamber," promised Rory. "Pan and I call this wood that - the old King is the darlingest pine-tree, and he's got twenty-four courtiers." They emerged suddenly into a wide clearing, where a ring of fine old pines surrounded an immense tree, covered with cones as big as babies' heads. They lay fallen among the scented pine-needles, too, and Rory called them the king's treasures and began to pick them up to burn with the Christmas log.[11]

Could this be the 'ring of fir trees' where Doreen Valiente's Great Aunt Nance used to go to "commune with the pixies"?[12]

---

9   Katherine Oldmeadow *Madcap Judy* (Collins, 1919) p. 223.
10 Katherine Oldmeadow *Princess Charming* (Collins, 1923) p. 139.
11 ibid. p. 256-257.
12 Philip Heselton *Doreen Valiente Witch* (The Doreen Valiente Foundation in association with the Centre for Pagan Studies, 2016) p. 6.

Closely linked to this feeling for Nature is an awareness of the existence of fairies. Katherine definitely believed that fairies were real, although she couldn't see them. Ian Stevenson wrote to me:

> *I am now convinced that she believed in fairies, and probably elves and wood-nymphs. She regularly refers to fairies, or "they" as one of her characters always says! I'm not sure that she ever saw one - and this may have frustrated her. In writing once about all different kinds of doors, KLO says: "Doors are wonderful things ... There is the Door into Fairyland - the most wonderful door of all - which one seeks and never finds ..." This is her own comment, not from one of her characters. ... She undoubtedly regarded Chewton Glen as a magical place, and she brings it into her books ...*[13]

And direct description by Katherine, strongly suggesting that she herself had experienced water-pixies in woodland pools, and accepted their existence, is the following: "... her eyes had that queer, deep, browny-green look seen in dark woodland pools usually inhabited by water-pixies ..."[14]

To take just one book, *Princess Charming* includes many references to fairies. There is also an extended passage which is the most vivid description of the spirit underlying Nature in any of Katherine Oldmeadow's writings. It is a story of girls setting up a school in somewhere very like The Glen House. There is much colourful description about the natural environment of The Glen, and about the fairies there:

> *... to be in a wood just after dawn with a girl who made an offering to the fairies thrilled her imagination, as she really believed in the Little People as firmly as did her old nurse, and to her every tree and flower in the Glen was haunted by the fairy folk.*

[13] Letter Ian Stevenson to the author 5 December 2000.
[14] Katherine Oldmeadow "The Witch of Whitestones" in *Hulton's Girls' Stories* (Allied Newspapers 1926) p. 144.

A fellow writer of children's books, Mabel Esther Allan, comments about Katherine Oldmeadow: "... as far as I can remember, there isn't a word about religion in any of the books."[15] This is certainly largely true of the Christian religion, as Ian Stevenson confirmed:

> *I spent seven years at boarding school and you couldn't ignore religion - morning and evening prayers, to church twice on Sundays. Yet KLO never seems to mention religion at her girls' boarding schools. There's talk and dressing up to do with mythological gods and goddesses - but no God with a capital G.*[16]

On looking through her books, I verified these comments. Divinity is represented almost exclusively by reference to Pagan gods and goddesses. There is hardly a mention of the Christian God, and no mention at all of Jesus, but there is a profusion of classical and other pagan deities. This is a very popular theme, particularly in *Princess Charming*:

> *"It's lucky we had classical dancing this term", said Nancy, "it will be jolly to have the nymphs barefoot, and those green Greek dresses will just do". ... "We must have twelve nymphs," said Barbara.*[17]

> *... in the middle of the door there swung an old copper knocker - the head of Pan, the woodland god, holding a round copper ring between his grinning lips.*[18]

> *"Let us have Greek statuary in the woods. There won't be a thing to learn, and we'll only have to get the dresses and practise the posing." ... "I thought we would make a little setting for the most well-known Grecian deities in the gardens and woods."*[19]

[15] Mabel Esther Allen "Ragged Robin Began It" in *Folly* No. 5 - January 1992.
[16] Letter Ian Stevenson to the author 5 December 2000.
[17] Katherine Oldmeadow *Madcap Judy* (Collins, 1919) p. 273.
[18] Katherine Oldmeadow *Princess Charming* (Collins, 1923) p. 101.
[19] ibid. pp. 142-143.

"I'll be Pan," announced Jill with determination. "I don't care if he is a boy. I simply love him, and I'm like him, too, because I adore wandering over mountains and rocks and woods and having people dance round me and teasing them." ... There in a little fern-grove, on the grassy knoll before a tall beech-tree, sat Jill, or rather Pan, for her small mischievous face against the background of greenery, her dark silky hair wreathed with leaves, and her expression of almost fiendish merriment was the very Pan of one's imagination. She was half-draped in a goat-skin, and in her brown, slender fingers she held a flute of reeds.[20]

———————————— •·◆◆·• ————————————

The Christian festivals of Easter and Christmas are hardly mentioned, but there is one festival which dominates the books - May Day. In Katherine Oldmeadow's books, these festivals are not imposed from above - the girls themselves have created them.

In her first book, *Madcap Judy*, are some very colourful descriptions of May Day celebrations:

A great, spreading, pink thorn-tree grew there, which would make a flowery and fragrant canopy for a May Queen. ... The evening before the birthday was spent in the woods, and the girls returned laden with wild flowers, and great branches of pink and white May ...[21]

Bettine, dressed as a wood-nymph, all in green, danced in with a crown of golden flowers, which she placed on the May Queen's head. Then very soft music sounded, and twelve nymphs in silver and green came running from the pine-wood in the distance, garlanded with flowers, six of them bearing great branches of white May, and six carrying Spring flowers of blue and gold.[22]

---

[20] ibid. pp. 144 and 152.
[21] Katherine Oldmeadow *Madcap Judy* pp. 276 and 278.
[22] ibid. p. 284.

And *Princess Anne* is largely centred on May Day:

> *At five o'clock the next morning Anne was awake, and because she liked doing pretty things as well as seeing and hearing them, she decided she would get up and wash her face in May dew, and pick a posy for the Queen of the May ... Last May Day, father had been with her, and she had made him wash his face in May dew, and afterwards they had sat on a rocky tor on Dartmoor, and father had told her about all the ancient rites of May.*[23]

> *"If we don't laugh on May Day, and make others laugh, and dance the winter out and the summer in, we shall all cry before the year's out." "Who said so?" demanded Elma. "Father did - he knew such lots of things about old May Day; he knew what all the old Morris dances meant, too, and heaps of things."*[24]

> *They joined hands and danced round the first oak tree they saw, because Anne Golden said it was a rite of May to dance round a tree - the most wonderful thing in Nature - clapping your hands with joy that it is green again.*[25]

> *It was decided that the Queen should be enthroned beneath a canopy of willow branches held by four of her maidens. ... Thirteen maidens stood in a semi-circle round the canopy, bearing hazel staves entwined with flowers and greenery...*[26]

Katherine Oldmeadow was obviously attuned to themes that we would today refer to as pagan, as early as her first book, published in 1919. Indeed, the previous year, while the First World War was still in progress, she put on a play she had written for children entitled *The Little Green Man*. It was performed in the open air, in the extensive grounds of Nea House, Highcliffe. It was subtitled *A Forest Legend* and included forest fairies, elves and village

---

[23] Katherine Oldmeadow *Princess Anne* pp. 200-201.
[24] ibid. p. 211.
[25] ibid. p. 214.
[26] ibid. pp. 215-216.

maidens. This was all well before the Sabines, the Chalks or the Masons came to the Christchurch area.

43. The cast of "The Little Green Man - A Forest Legend" by Katherine Oldmeadow performed in the grounds of Nea House, Highcliffe 1918

Before going into more detail on other aspects of Katherine Old-meadow's books, I will mention an observation that well-known authority on witchcraft and paganism, Professor Ronald Hutton, made after reading a draft of my earlier book, *Gerald Gardner and the Cauldron of Inspiration*. He wrote:

> *I wonder if you underestimate the quantity of classically-based paganism and nature-worship which infused lettered English culture in general by the early twentieth century. As Oldmeadow herself says, references to classical deities, with little or no Christian imagery, are scattered throughout Elizabethan verse, as through that of lyrical poets ever since, and the work of Chaucer long before. May is the main festival mentioned in the same poetry, and in Chaucer, rather than Easter or Christmas, and also (since the late Victorian revival of Merry England) the main one actually celebrated within girls' schools ...*[27]

---

[27] Letter Ronald Hutton to the author 11 August 2001.

I have no reason to doubt that Professor Hutton is right in that such topics as classically-based paganism and nature worship were common amongst a certain type of writer of the early 20th Century and that in themselves they in no way demonstrate that Katherine Oldmeadow was involved in a pre-existing tradition of witchcraft.

But what if we turn the whole argument on its head? What if the themes present in her writings were actually the origin of parts of what, in the late 1930s, became the witch cult that Gerald Gardner encountered?

Did Katherine Oldmeadow, alone, or more likely in combination with others, weave the themes which she wrote about into a newly-conceived and emerging witch cult?

If one considers these possibilities, it opens up the potential for putting a whole new emphasis on Katherine Oldmeadow's words and when she wrote them. With this in mind, let us look at some of her other themes.

16
An Occult Imagination

In Katherine Oldmeadow's books there is a strong awareness of the world underlying physical reality, including mention of various methods of divination, such as witch balls and scrying mirrors, dream books and dowsing, as well as a belief in numerology.

She refers to the witch mirror, used for scrying ('far-seeing') in the same way as a crystal ball, and that some girls seemed to have the ability to use them.

> *"Surely you've heard of witchs' mirrors and crystal balls that you can gaze into and see the future? And every one knows Queen Elizabeth kept a pet astrologer or magician to look into a mirror for her. Didn't your aunt say yours might have belonged to a queen? As a matter of fact I believe it belonged to Queen Elizabeth." "But who can see the future in it now?" "I can." Louise spoke solemnly, and a cold shiver crept down Elizabeth's spine. "And I can see the past, and the present, too."*

> *"Of course most people wouldn't see anything in your mirror but their own reflections," went on Louise, "but I'm 'fey' - always have been - and if I like to give my mind to it I can see anything - in the right sort of glass."*

> *Elizabeth had heard of Queen Elizabeth's superstitious dabblings in astrology, and of her belief in reading the future in crystal balls, and in a flash she remembered her first visit to the House with the Red Door, when her aunt had told her to go and examine the many curious things on her table. She had taken up a worn leather case which contained a cracked glass, and Aunt Mary had smiled and said, "That was called a Witch's Mirror in the seventeenth century," but to hear that there were people in the world*

now who could see the future in mirrors startled her but thrilled her too.[1]

This is so specific that I suspect that Katherine Oldmeadow knew someone who had such a mirror and knew how to use it. And I strongly suspect that Elizabeth's reaction was a reflection of what Katherine herself felt when she came across this.

An extended part of *Princess Candida* is about the Delphic Oracle and the schoolgirls' imitation of it, and there are other divinatory techniques in several of the books:

> *Then she played her favourite game of shutting her eyes and putting her finger on the page, just to see if the words fitted the moment.*[2]

> *I put all the school prospectuses on the floor in a ring, and then pointed Peter Moone's cutlass at them with my eyes shut. It stopped at King's Corner.*[3] This was the school that she decided to go to.

Princess Elizabeth includes much on numerology:

> *"I'm silly, I know - but what is numerology?" "It's a sort of cult" (Elizabeth was no wiser.) "and a tremendously ancient one - I believe the Egyptians believed in it. By studying certain numbers you can find out in which element you were born - Fire, Air or Water, and from that you can find out which days and months are particularly lucky to you."*[4]

This is interesting in that it misses out the element of Earth, as we have seen that Rosamund did in her article, 'Rose of the World'.[5]

Also, Gerald Gardner writes of the group into which he was initiated:

---

[1] Katherine Oldmeadow *Princess Elizabeth* (Collins, 1926) pp. 171-172.
[2] Katherine Oldmeadow *Princess Anne* (Collins, 1925) p. 248.
[3] Katherine Oldmeadow (writing as Pamela Grant) *The Fortunes of Billy* (Collins, 1925) p. 58.
[4] Katherine Oldmeadow *Princess Elizabeth* (Collins, 1926) p. 150.
[5] see Chapter 9.

The cult seems to use a crude numerology - whence obtained I do not know. The numbers 3, 5, 8, 13 and 40 are thought good or lucky and all these numbers have significance attached to them.[6]

And, as we have seen, Rosamund used numerology, for example in connection with the significance of the petals on the rose.

Secret societies and initiation rituals feature prominently in Katherine Oldmeadow's works. And, of course, the witch cult and its development into Wicca is a secret society with secret initiation rituals and corresponding significant sayings and initials. Katherine was not alone in introducing secret societies into her school stories: they were one of the staple elements in such books. The names of the societies in her books include the Secret Seven [*Madcap Judy*], also known as the SSSS; the Black Brotherhood [*The Pimpernel Patrol*]; the Society of School Savages (SSS) and the Bad Brownies Brigade (BBB) [*The Fortunes of Billy*]; the Red Circle [*Princess Elizabeth*] and the Boys' Brigade (BB) [*The Fortunes of Jacky*]. Note the preponderance of two initials, B and S, which even extends to the initials of some of the main characters, such as Bill Briggs, the hero of *The Fortunes of Jacky*[7] and Susan Silvertrees, the heroine of *When George III was King*.[8]

There are also initiation ceremonies which include much archaic language, so, for example, we get:

"Behold!" said Judy. "if thou art really true, and wish to join the Secret Seven (it simply can't be Eight, or everything's spoilt), take this deadly instrument and plunge it into thine arm, and with the blood that flows, write thy initials on this brave scroll."[9]

"Tis well," cried Judy; "truly thou art a sport" and as she waved her hand the Secret Seven clapped softly. If you

---

[6] Gardner (1954) p. 114.

[7] Katherine Oldmeadow *The Fortunes of Jacky* (The Children's Press, 1957).

[8] Katherine Oldmeadow *When George III was King* (Hutchinson, 1934).

[9] Katherine Oldmeadow *Madcap Judy* (Collins, 1919) p. 58.

prove true during the next seven suns, thou shalt receive the badge of the SSSS, and also we will initiate thee into the signs, and our secret language, and then thou shalt be an active member".[10]

"Sisters must swear never to divulge the Secrets of the Society."[11]

The Seven rising, marched solemnly around Jean's bed seven times ...[12]

Judy solemnly made the sign of an 'S' in the air.[13]

At this speech, the SSS made mysterious signs - which were maddening to the uninitiated.[14]

Ritual elements such as dancing barefoot and the use of candles, wands and knives are referred to frequently. As Ian Stevenson comments: *KLO clearly liked to be close to nature and I am sure she felt closest when she went barefooted. In different books, she has girl characters who do this. I think one of the attractions of gypsies to KLO was that they lived close to nature, with the children going shoeless.[15]* To give just a few examples:

They disappeared into the glades of the Forest, where Diana, immediately taking off her shoes, hung them round her neck. It was delicious to race on the springy turf ...[16]

Elizabeth longed to take off her thick shoes and stockings and walk in the long grass barefoot ...[17]

---

[10] ibid. p. 58.

[11] ibid. p. 74.

[12] ibid. p. 59.

[13] ibid. p. 71.

[14] *The Fortunes of Billy* (1925) p. 213.

[15] Ian Stevenson, letter to the author, 5 December 2000.

[16] *Madcap Judy* (1919) p. 229.

[17] *Princess Elizabeth* (1926) p. 53.

Other ritual activities mentioned include:

> "... *our fingers are ten magic wands given to us by the fairies*"... *she liked the idea of the magic wand so much that she thought she would try her power in using one* ...[18]

> ... *they provided themselves with fresh birch rods from the woods with such delight that Dorothy wondered if she had been wise in advising a St. Nicholas revel.*[19]

There are clearly several themes which are now part of modern pagan witchcraft: scrying, divination, numerology, initiation rituals and dancing barefoot, to name but a few. If Katherine Oldmeadow were part of the group which eventually initiated Gerald Gardner, I feel she would undoubtedly have participated in the development of beliefs and practices which would have included these elements.

However, there is one topic in Katherine's writings which we have so far neglected, but which has proved particularly interesting and revealing: that of witchcraft.

---

[18]   Katherine Oldmeadow *Princess Candida* (Collins, 1922) p. 257.
[19]   *Princess Charming* (1923) p. 247.

17
Witchcraft and Encounters
on the Common

Of particular interest is Katherine Oldmeadow's mention of witchcraft, as I think I spot something very interesting happening, which is that her attitude to witches and witchcraft changes markedly between her earlier and later books.

In her earlier books most of the mentions are negative, describing witchcraft in terms of something to be feared. For example:

> "If we find Miss Miranda is a witch, we must tell the vicar, and he will have her ducked as an example to the other witches ..."[1]

> It was a warm, misty night. "Just the night for witches," Judy said, which gave Jean another shiver.[2]

> ... she hated the gipsy woman with the gray beard, she was so like a witch.[3]

> ... she hated going to be alone, with a witch living under the staircase![4]

> "She's a witch, you know. If you poked your nose through that door which leads into her part of the house, she'll cast an awful spell on you."[5]

Whenever witches are mentioned in the earlier books, they are referred to in such terms.

---

[1] *Madcap Judy* (1919) p. 148.
[2] ibid. p. 151.
[3] *Ragged Robin* (1920) p. 22.
[4] ibid. p. 93.
[5] *Princess Anne* (1925) p. 156.

However, a change seems to occur in about 1925-1926. After that time, witchcraft is shown in a more positive light. This can be seen with reference to ash trees. In 1925, she was writing : "They crossed their thumbs as they fled past the stunted ash tree near the stone wall, because Juanita said a witch lived in every ash tree."[6]

By the following year there is a very much more positive attitude to witches and witchcraft. In one story, 'The Witch of White-stones', Billy, a girl who pretends to be a witch, says that "ash trees are fearfully witchy, you know" and holds "a long conversation with the ash-trees."[7] This was a long time before most people had ever heard of "talking to trees"!

The early writings refer to witch balls as keeping witches away:

> *"We used to have splendiferous times, too," said Jean Macdonald. "Dad's got a witch's ball." "A witch's ball, what's that?" asked Bobby. "The rummiest thing. It's all colours, and you hang it up outside over the doorway on All Hallows' Eve, and it keeps away the witches."[8]*

However, this changes with her later writings:

> *"Oh, look! There's a witch's ball!" She pointed to a large, silver ball. The words on the card attached to it were, "Genuine crystal Ball. Will keep off the Evil Eye."[9]*

> *... very likely would hang among them a witch's glass ball, a gaudy thing with coloured stripes that must never be dusted and was considered marvellous for keeping off the evil eye.[10]*

These are positive statements about witch balls, making it clear that those who used them (who must have been witches because

---

6   ibid. p. 214.
7   Katherine Oldmeadow 'The Witch of Whitestones' in *Hulton's Girls' Stories* (Allied Newspapers 1926) p. 144.
8   *Ragged Robin* (1920) p. 144.
9   *The Three Mary Anns* (Cassell 1948) p. 104.
10 *The Folklore of Herbs* (1946) p. 24.

they were witch balls) were afforded protection against the "evil eye", rather than against witchcraft.

A down-to-earth attitude to witchcraft appears to be firmly established by the time *When George III was King* was published in 1934. When one of the heroines of the story, which is set at the time of the threatened Napoleonic invasion, was asked what she would like to be, she replied that she wanted to be a travel writer, but that because she was a girl, she couldn't, and she would have to stay at home:

> *"But I shan't be only a housewife," continued Charlotte. "I shall be a witch too."*
>
> *"A witch! Oh, Charlotte, but witches are wicked!" cried Susan in distress.*
>
> *"Not a white witch ... They are wise old women and know all about herbs that heal. I shall learn Latin, and study plants and herbs, and grow them in the garden and make them into medicines and ointments for Father's patients. I shall be a wise young woman ..."* [11]
>
> *... "You can't be a white witch and a wise woman unless you understand all about herbs..."* [12]

Katherine Oldmeadow also writes other interesting positive things about witches in *The Folklore of Herbs*, which seem to demonstrate a familiarity with witchcraft. She was certainly sufficiently aware by 1926 to know that there were witches who healed. She calls them "white witches", and there are extended passages in *The Folklore of Herbs* where she makes a clear distinction between 'white' and 'black' witches, after which she makes a very interesting statement:

> *The white witch of today still holds queer beliefs about mixing creatures with her simple medicines ...* [13]

[11] *When George III was King* (1934) pp. 22-24.

[12] ibid. p. 61.

[13] *The Folklore of Herbs* p. 15.

This is a very clear statement which implies that witches still existed when she was writing and that she knew at least one of them sufficiently well to know what they believed. She states that "witches always had herb gardens", a very definite statement which implies that she knew some who did.

Her continuing distinction between 'white' and 'black' witches clearly demonstrates that she was aware that there are witches who do not do harm (presumably because she had personal knowledge of them) and wanted to distinguish them from the 'other kind'. This distinction is totally absent from her pre-1926 books, which refer to witchcraft in purely negative terms.

What caused Katherine Oldmeadow's sudden change of approach to witchcraft? Could it be that she met someone in about 1925 who caused her to change her opinions? Someone who healed people through the use of herbs? Someone who revealed to Katherine that she was a witch.

There is one, and only one person who meets these criteria, and that person is Rosamund Sabine.

———————————————

Chewton Common is one of the range of commons which lie between the New Forest and the coast, usually on poorer quality land. It is, however, an area which has been subject to encroachment by suburban development in settlements such as Walkford and Highcliffe. The map forming Illustration 33 shows the situation as it was in 1939.

The Common features in what seems to be a joke either by Gerald or at his expense. He writes in *Witchcraft Today*:

> *They* [the witches] ... *tell me that in most villages the witches arranged that the first and last house was occupied by a member of the cult, and any strange witch, travelling*

or 'on the run', could go where she would be sure of help and protection.[14]

Realistically, even in a period with little new housing development on the outskirts of villages, this would have been very difficult to arrange, and certainly not something to rely on in a time of persecution.

So, where did this most implausible idea originate? I think someone was looking at the map of Highcliffe one day and noticed that the Mill House, the Glen House and Whinchat (homes of the Fordhams, the Oldmeadows and the Sabines) were all right on the edge of the village and therefore all could be considered the first (or last) house. At some point, someone noticed this and made a joke of it, perhaps fooling Gerald into taking it seriously, or perhaps he was in on it or even originated the joke himself. It certainly confirms his comment that witches are good leg-pullers, which is on the same page of *Witchcraft Today*.

Katherine, in The Glen House, and Rosamund, in Whinchat, were living barely half a mile apart. We know that they both had a deep interest in herbs and would therefore explore the nearest wild uncultivated land to seek out herbal supplies. Particularly if one or both had dogs that needed taking for a walk, it is highly likely that some time relatively soon after Rosamund had moved into the area, in early 1925, they would have met on the Common and would have realised fairly quickly that they shared common interests which were not just confined to herbs.

They were both interested in the deeper, more spiritual, side of herbalism and would, I am sure, quickly got on to conversing on more esoteric topics.

At some stage, and I imagine that it would be by the end of 1925, Rosamund revealed to Katherine that she was a witch, or, as she might have put it, 'a white witch'.

---

[14] Gardner (1954) p. 54.

By 1946, when Katherine's only non-fiction book, *The Folklore of Herbs*, was published, her interest in herbs was obviously well-established. She had written an article entitled 'A Herb Garden in Wartime', which is clearly about her own abundant and well-stocked herb garden. It starts:

> *How completely did Providence guard against boredom in the days before speed became our master! Preserves, cordials, wines, perfumes, cosmetics were nearly all made at home, and it was the duty of the good housekeeper to see that the medicine-chest was stocked as well as the store-cupboard. To achieve this she must tend and watch over the herbs in her garden, and these included the plain and unadorned - those pot and physic herbs worth their weight in gold to the skilled herbalist.*
>
> *She must also keep a watchful eye on the hedgerows, for she had been wisely taught that all herbs especially beneficial to mankind are prolific and appear at a time when most needed.*[15]

We have already looked at Rosamund's interest and the Culpeper, box of drawers and herbalist's equipment which she possessed.

It is possible that the Common was used for rituals as late as the early 1950s (i.e. before the publication of *Witchcraft Today*). Author, the late Michael Hodges, told me:

> *In my youth at New Milton, where I was in the Scouts, I was told by another boy (circa 1950) of a boy at Highcliffe who had seen nude women dancing in a circle around a tree at Chewton Common. He had told his father, who had not believed him. However, he took his father to the site, where they found a necklace on the ground.*[16]

This report is, of course, very indirect, but it is, nevertheless, intriguing.

---

[15] Katherine Oldmeadow - 'A Herb Garden in Wartime' in *My Garden - An Intimate Magazine for Garden Lovers* No. 118 (October 1943) pp 297-301

[16] Michael Hodges - personal communication with the author.

.

.

18
Elspeth Begg and Witch Ancestry

I first came across the name Elspeth Begg in a letter from Gerald Gardner to Cecil Williamson, while Gerald was spending the winter of 1953-1954 with his friend Denis Collings in Achimota, Gold Coast (now Ghana). He writes:

> ... I got a very fine Toad Stone Ring. Elspeth Begg was after it, but I beat her by a short head.[1]

This sounds like it was some sort of auction which they both attended.

She was obviously interested in unusual rings, as she lent a ring to Gerald Gardner's museum. The caption reads:

> This ring has been in the Earl of Lonsdale's family for some 300 years. It was the tooth of some animal as its principal, supposed to have mystic power over its possessor. It is set around with stones to insure its potency.[2]

Gerald had probably known her for at least 15 years, for at the first meeting of the Folklore Society which he attended, on 15th March 1939, she signed the attendance book immediately before Gerald, and this was repeated at several subsequent meetings. I think it's reasonable to assume that they came together.

In fact, she first attended the meetings on 19th January 1938, signing in as "E.J. Begg, Bournemouth, Hants." By November 1938 she was a member, giving her address as "c/o The Westminster Bank, Boscombe".

---

[1] Letter from Gerald Gardner to Cecil Williamson 23 December 1953 (Document 89 Boscastle Museum of Witchcraft archives).
[2] Museum caption in the Toronto collection.

Looking at the Register which was taken in September 1939, I could find no sign of an Elspeth Begg, but I did find an Elsie J Begg, living at Harcourt, 15 Derby Road, Bournemouth, living with an Alice J Begg, her mother. They were both living on private means.

Gerald Gardner's letter to Cecil Williamson was in fact the only occasion that the name Elspeth was used, and I suspect that it was his 'nickname' for her based on his knowledge of Scottish witchcraft history, as we shall see.

In 1941, E J Begg wrote a piece in the journal *Folk Lore* on the subject of 'Cases of Witchcraft in Dorsetshire'.[3] It is a note of less than three pages under the general heading of 'Collectanea'. She tells seven tales of witchcraft in Dorset and starts the note:

> *The following stories of witchcraft in Dorsetshire were all told to me recently. My informant was a farmer, Mr. Bacon of Woodlands, Dorset, and he told me that all the tales were "perfectly true".*[4]

Information in the article, including his age, enables her informer to be identified as Harold E. Bacon of Burgess Farm.

The examples given in the article are all reasonably local to Verwood and include such themes as shapeshifting into a hare, horses ridden at night and gypsy curses.

Now, "Elspeth Begg" is an interesting name. It refers to a character implicated in the story of Janet Horne, the last person to be burnt as a witch in Scotland, in 1727. There are few references to her (for example, neither Margaret Murray[5] nor Arnold Crowther[6] mention her.) but I suspect that at some stage Elsie had heard about her (perhaps following an interest in family history) and decided to adopt the name. Then again, it could just be Gerald's

---

3 *Folk Lore* vol lii pp. 70-72.
4 ibid. p. 70.
5 Margaret Alice Murray *The Witch-Cult in Western Europe* (Oxford 1921).
6 Arnold Crowther *Witchcraft and the Scots* (The Doreen Valiente Foundation in association with the Centre for Pagan Studies, 2018).

appellation, just as when he called Edith Dafo. He had become very knowledgeable about magic and witchcraft and his library contained more than one book on Scottish witchcraft.[7]

Rona Munro wrote a play entitled *The Last Witch*, which was performed for the first time in 2009.[8] In the play, Elspeth Begg, who is a neighbour of Janet Horne, the witch who is executed, remains sympathetic to her and there is a strong implication that she is a witch herself.

Nine years after this execution, the act which made witchcraft a capital offence was repealed.

Bob Trubshaw has written a short story[9] about a suggested meeting between Gerald Gardner and Alexander Keiller, the marmalade manufacturer and benefactor of archaeological excavations at Avebury. He postulates that "Elsie Begg" is a pseudonym for Edith Woodford-Grimes. It is certainly true that Edith used "Elsie" as a pseudonym, but I have demonstrated that Elsie Begg was a real person. I have found her dates of birth and death and where she was living in 1939. But Bob has written a good story and he draws attention as to where Gardner obtained the witch-name Morven for the witch in his novel *High Magic's Aid*.[10]

Elsie Jennie Begg was born on 2nd September 1897 in Assam, Bengal to Alice Jane and Robert John Begg, who was a tea planter. In about 1901 the family moved to England and in March of that year were living at 258 Portsdown Road, Paddington, London. Elsie (her middle name was now given as "Jeanie") was aged 3 and she had a baby brother named John. Robert was only 42 when they moved to England. As well as "tea planter", for which there was

[7] J W Brodie-Innes *Scottish Witchcraft Trials* (The Chiswick Press, 1891); Charles Kirkpatrick Sharpe *A Historical Account of the Belief of Witchcraft in Scotland* (Hamilton Adams & Co., Thomas D Morrison, 1884); R Burns Begg *Trials for Witchcraft in Scotland in 1661 and 1662.*

[8] Rona Munro *The Last Witch* (Nick Hern Books, 2009).

[9] Bob Trubshaw *Halloween 1938* in http://www.indigogroup.co.uk/avebury/story01.htm

[10] Scire (G B Gardner) *High Magic's Aid* (Michael Houghton, 1949).

presumably not much demand in Paddington, his occupation is given as 'Grocer'.

Robert died in 1926 and I suspect that shortly after that date Elsie and her mother moved to The Lawn, Church Road, Bournemouth and, some time after 1932, to the house at 15 Derby Road where they were in 1939. Alice died in 1958 and Elsie in 1975.

As to whether Elsie was ever a member of what we might call the coven, we really don't know, but Gerald Gardner writes in *The Meaning of Witchcraft* that:

> ... *I know personally of three people in one coven who discovered that, subsequent to their coming into the cult in this life, their ancestors had links with it ...*[11]

I don't know the extent to which Elsie had found that she was a direct descendent of the historical Elspeth Begg, but she may have felt an emotional link just as Gerald felt a link with Grissel Gairdner, although no factual link has ever been demonstrated.

It is, I think, interesting that Gerald apparently knew Elsie Begg at least six months before he claims to have been initiated. However, she did not feature in any of the Crotona Fellowship activities, so how did he get to know her?

---

[11]   G B Gardner *The Meaning of Witchcraft* (Aquarian, 1959) p 14

19

Irene Lyon Clark, Druidry and the Sword of Nuada

When visiting a museum it is usually the objects on display which catch one's attention rather than the dusty archive, frequently hidden in attic or basement, which often comes along with it.

I have mostly found archives to be fascinating and informative, however, and essential for carrying out my research for this and previous books. Occasionally, however, it is indeed the artefacts which take centre stage, as in the case of the ritual sword which was the pride of Gerald Gardner's collection.

The issue of provenance is an important one in the world of antiques, in other words knowing where the object came from. Indeed, we cannot always rely on museum captions or guide books, as the writer of these descriptions would not necessarily always know where they originated.

Take the example of the sword. This is currently in the possession of the North London coven, which is the continuation of the Bricket Wood coven founded by Gerald Gardner. I have had the privilege of seeing, handling and photographing it, and I give an extended description of it in my book *Gerald Gardner and the Cauldron of Inspiration*[1], but in essence it consists of an old sword blade, with a guard and pommel based closely on the illustration contained in Mathers' *Key of Solomon*, first published in 1888. There are, however, certain additions, a pentagram on the pommel with a Druid symbol inside it. (See Illustration 46).

---

[1] Philip Heselton (2003) pp. 89-95.

The current owners of the sword believe it to have been Dafo's. I think the truth is more likely to have been that it ended up with her and that she was the one who finally passed it to Gardner. As with all the artefacts which were passed to Gerald, Dafo had been the intermediary.

I had at first thought that the sword had been owned by Rosamund Sabine, but I am far less certain of that now. Rosamund had applied for membership of the Golden Dawn offshoot, the Rectified Rite, founded by A. E. Waite, and Grevel Lindop drew my attention to the absence of swords in A.E. Waite's Fellowship of the Rosy Cross. It seems to me quite probable that they weren't emphasised in his Rectified Rite either.

Moreover, there seems to be a definite link between the sword and the Ancient Druid Order. And it seems to me now that the original owner of the sword was most likely Irene Lyon Clark.

Irene Margaret Lyon Clark (1899-1947), an artist and designer of theatrical costumes, could well have been the first member of the Ancient Druid Order that Gardner had met, for she had been an active member of the Crotona Fellowship, performing in several of their plays and designing and making most of their costumes. She had been born on 28th November 1899, at Walsingham in Norfolk, the daughter of Minnie Ellen Guy and her husband, William Guy, the schoolmaster in the village.

Walsingham has long been a place of pilgrimage since, in the year 1081, Richeldis de Faverches had a vision of the Virgin Mary, who told her to build a replica of the Holy House in Nazareth. The village remains a place of Anglican and Catholic pilgrimage to this day. Other denominations are also represented, including the Russian Orthodox church, which has converted the former railway station.

So, a background of immersion in ritual of various types seems likely for Irene.

On 10th November 1928, she married William L Lyon Clark (1858-1934) in Chelsea, south-west London. He was born in Aston in Warwickshire and spent his early life in India and South Africa. In 1880 he managed a tea estate in Badapur, Assam. Irene was his third wife, his two previous marriages ended, the first in death and the second in divorce. For some reason, he changed his name by deed poll in 1911 from William Lyon Clark to William Lyon Lyon-Clark. He died in the south of France in 1934.

44. Irene Lyon-Clark with her husband, William

By 1937, Irene was living in the Christchurch area, and she was writing articles for the *Christchurch Times* on 'Literary Links with Christchurch'.[2]

She was also clearly by that time a member of the Crotona Fellowship, as she had 'RcB' after her name - a Rosicrucian qualification. To start with, she lived at Ballard Lodge, New Milton, probably having some connection with Great Ballard School. She later had a bungalow built in Somerford near to the Ashrama and Theatre.

---

[2] *Christchurch Times* 9 and 16 October 1937.

It is clear that Gerald Gardner knew her well while they were both attending the Crotona Fellowship meetings. He also kept in touch with her after the war as they both attended a meeting of the Ancient Druid Order in Leamington Spa at the Winter Solstice 1946.

Less than a year after this, however, Irene died in Ipswich on 17th December 1947 at the comparatively young age of 48. The 1951 issue of the Druid magazine, *The Double Circle* was dedicated "to the memory of our esteemed companion Irene Lyon Clarke [sic]".

45. Irene Lyon-Clark (on right)

Whilst her will does not mention any ritual items specifically, it is quite likely that she would have arranged to pass these on to another Druid who would appreciate them for what they represented. I am sure that Gardner would have both appreciated and coveted the sword during that period.

Irene's death, just 17 days after that of Aleister Crowley, caught Gardner out of the country visiting his brother in the USA, but it was a period when he was enthusiastically adopting ritual magic, into which the sword would most definitely fit.

Gerald certainly had the sword in his possession by 1951 because he wrote to Cecil Williamson:

> *The Druids wrote as they [want] me to come to Stonehenge this Midsummer +they hinted they could borrow the Sword ... again. ... I know it's the only one that exactly fits the hole in the stone + it has a sheath, + they must have a sheath for the ceremony.*[3]

The Guide to the Museum of Magic and Witchcraft, published in 1958, connects the sword with the collection of objects for herb preparation. It says:

> *She had a very fine ritual sword, which for many years was lent to the Druid Order which holds the annual Midsummer ceremony at Stonehenge, because it fitted exactly into the cleft in the Hele Stone.*[4]

The Guide was written by Doreen Valiente at Gardner's direction, and the conflation of the two descriptions, of the collection and the sword, may be the result of her misinterpretation of what Gardner had told her.

It is possible that Irene, who was described in *The Double Circle* as "esteemed", was a member of the secretive inner circle of the Druid Order, the Nuada Temple.

---

[3] Letter Gerald Gardner to Cecil Williamson late April 1951 in Boscastle Museum of Witchcraft collection.

[4] G. B. Gardner (1958) p. 15.

46. The sword pommel showing both Druid and Witch symbols

Gardner writes about the Sword of Nuada as being one of the four magical talismans which the Tuatha de Danaan brought to Ireland. He says:

> ... the Sword of Nuada, "from whose stroke no one ever escaped or recovered", is none other than the sword of the Old God of Death Himself, which is yet borne symbolically by His representative in the rites of witchcraft.[5]

This seems to indicate that the sword was both a Druid and a witch sword and that, if so, it seems likely that Irene Lyon Clark was also both a Druid and a witch.

---

5 Gardner (1959) p. 124.

47. The sword hilt with pentagram disc

20

The Emergence of the Rose

This chapter is, in large part, conjecture. In it, I examine some of the interests of our group and how they might have combined to become the seed out of which the witch cult into which Gerald Gardner was initiated might have emerged, not fully formed, but a true ancestor of what today is often called Wicca.

So far, we have identified several people who may have been members of the group into which Gardner was initiated. Those individuals include Edith Rose Woodford Grimes ('Dafo'); Susie, Ernie and Rosetta Mason; Dorothy St. Quintin Fordham ('Old Dorothy'); Katherine Louise Oldmeadow; Catherine Chalk; Mabel Besant Scott; Elsie Begg; Irene Lyon Clark; and Rosamund and George Sabine.

Initially this was not a group who met together, but a network or very loose grouping of people with esoteric and other interests. The range of interests of this group of individuals, both mundane and esoteric, needs to be looked at in more detail, but let us summarise what we now know about these individuals, including how they earned their livings.

Edith was a teacher of speech and drama, as well as English literature. Later she became a professional teacher of elocution. The Masons were all part of the family firm, which involved making colour slides. Ernie was an enthusiastic amateur astronomer, having an observatory in his garden and a workshop where he ground lenses and prepared chemical concoctions. Katherine Oldmeadow was, of course, a writer of stories who also had a great interest in nature, particularly herbs, an interest which she shared with Rosamund. She shared an interest in folklore with Elsie

Begg. Catherine Chalk was interested in the history of theatre, as well as being a trained singer and song-writer.

And this was all before we come to their esoteric interests, which include the Golden Dawn and its offshoots; Co-Masonry; Theosophy; Druidry; astrology and Eastern disciplines such as yoga.

In fact, let us take yoga as an example. It is a very popular discipline nowadays but was far less so in the early years of the 20th Century, though it was the subject of attention by the Theosophical Society.

Gerald Gardner was aware of his new friends' interest in the subject, for Bracelin writes in the context of Gardner's understanding of what their secret consisted: *He still thought they might be mooting Yoga, or something of that nature.*[1] This suggests that yoga had been mentioned sufficiently often for him to think this a possibility.

And when Gardner was writing the manuscript which became *Witchcraft Today*, he had initially included quite a lot on yoga. Gerald Yorke, who worked for the publishers, Rider and Co., obviously decided that this was not really relevant to the subject of the book. Gardner replied to his comments: *I've cut the yoga.*

There are other hints that the wica (as Gerald's new friends eventually revealed that they were called) were interested in yoga. Edith's grandson told me that she regularly carried out yoga postures in the nude. Also, a second-hand volume called *Advanced Course in Yogi Philosophy* was advertised on the internet as being by Katherine Oldmeadow. I am certain that this is, in fact, the volume by Yogi Ramacharaka (a pseudonym of William Walker Atkinson)[2] and that Katherine had put her signature in the book merely because she owned it. It does, however, show an interest

---

[1] Bracelin p. 165.
[2] Yogi Ramacharaka *Advanced Course in Yogi Philosophy and Oriental Occultism* (Fowler, 1905).

in yoga on her part also, covering more than just the physical aspects.

Was the rose of special significance to the witches that Gardner knew? Or am I making too much of what is, after all, an English obsession, or certainly was so eighty years ago, and has many associations in folklore, religion and in other spheres.

Dorothy's commonplace books show that, not only was the rose her favourite flower, but she liked to use rose imagery, sometimes in cases where it really wasn't appropriate, almost as if she was trying to get reference to roses into every bit of poetry she could:

> *Now, the garden is a Blaze*
> *With the Queen of all the Days*
> *Rainbows coming back in June*
> *Roses that are gone too soon*
> *But of every flower that grows*
> *Lovely perfect English Rose.* [9 June 1942]

> *Roses on the Pergola and Roses in the bed*
> *Roses pink and white and yellow, Roses too of Red*
> *What a feast of colour, what a scent divine*
> *The best time of the summer is just*
> *The Rose's Time.* [1 June 1942]

> *Queen Rose of the Rosebud*
> *Garden of Girls, Queen Lily and Rose in one....*
> *And know you as the Queen*
> *Of the loveliest of Roses*
> *This world has ever seen.* [1 June 1943]

> *If you had only just the shape*
> *And form and colour rare*
> *You'd say there never had been made*
> *A flower half so fair, but when you had the extra gift*
> *The Scent with which it goes*

> *There's nothing so perfect on this Earth*
> *As the .... Perfect Rose.* [23 June 1943]

With regard to names, apart from Rosamund, we have Rosetta Mason, her daughter Rosetta, Edith's middle name, Rose, and her daughter, Rosanne.

Of course, the Rose was part of the Rosicrucian symbol of the rose and the cross.

Most of those individuals we have identified as being part of the witch cult had connections, both direct and indirect, with the Rosicrucian Order Crotona Fellowship.

It seems to me at least a possibility that a group of individuals within the Crotona Fellowship had become dissatisfied with the way it was going. Of the two great symbols of Rosicrucianism, the rose and the cross, they wanted more emphasis on the rose. Ostensibly, this was supposed to represent the Virgin Mary, but I think our group saw it more generally as the feminine principle and the pagan or universal approach rather than the Christian.

Rosamund's 1930 article related the petals of the rose with the sacred numbers, and books appeared like *The Rose Immortal* by the Co-Mason, Aimée Bothwell Gosse, first published in 1916. Its foreword by Ralph Shirley puts the rose in context:

> *The Rose has linked together East and West, being recognized by all alike as a symbol of the Path towards Divine Perfection as well as of the Goal of Attainment itself. The particular significance of the Rose has varied in the language of the mystics according to its colour. Thus the Red Rose, the White Rose, the Golden Rose, and the Black Rose have each their special connotations; while variations of meaning are drawn from the number and arrangement of the petals and the essence and fragrance of the perfume.*

> *To the great Saints and Seers the Rose has ever been the symbol of Divine Union, while to those who are in an earlier stage of the Divine Adventure it speaks in the first place of mingled joy and sorrow. The Rose being the Flower of Flowers, naturally represents the greatest gift of God to*

man - the knowledge of Himself. The union of the Rose and the Cross in the symbol of the Rosicrucians indicates that Divine Perfection can be attained through Love and Suffering alone.[3]

It may well be that our group was initially a reaction to the male dominated esoteric environment which they were faced with in Rosicrucianism. I think in time a rose goddess such as Aphrodite may have emerged as an integrating symbol for them.

There is an unusual phrase in the Lammas ritual of the witches, as passed down by Gerald Gardner. This is the phrase "by thy rosey love". Some such as the Farrars[4] were tempted to change this to "by the rose of thy love" but I think the original is correct and dates back to at least the 1930s when the group was coalescing. It is perhaps significant that Dorothy always used the spelling "rosey" in her commonplace books rather than the far more common "rosy".

Secrecy is also associated with the rose, and the term 'sub rosa' (beneath the rose) meant something that was secret. Also, a woman's vulva has been likened to a rose, and this may have been a very secret recognition by the group, who were, of course, mostly women.

I am aware that this section on the rose is extremely sketchy and I am currently investigating in more detail the extent to which the rose was a common feature for those who gradually formed the group into which Gerald Gardner was able to be initiated.

---

3   Aimée Bothwell Gosse *The Rose Immortal* (Rider, 1916) pp. 6-7.
4   Janet and Stewart Farrar *Eight Sabbats for Witches* (Hale, 1981) p. 113.

21

Witch Blood, Reincarnation and the Birth of the Witch Cult

Reincarnation was widely accepted as a natural process by those in occult and esoteric circles and is a major theme of both Theosophy and Rosicrucianism.

Gerald Gardner certainly accepted reincarnation, probably encouraged by his exposure to Buddhism and other philosophies during his working life out East.

Following his retirement in 1936 he began to have memories of a previous life in Cyprus, which were intensified following his visit to that island the following year.

He says that the verse entitled 'The Witch Recalls her last Incarnation', which is reproduced in *Witchcraft Today*,[1] came from a witch's book in his possession. He did not know who wrote it, but his use of the phrase 'The Witch' makes it likely that the book originally belonged to Edith Woodford Grimes.

In fact, the verse is an extract from the poem 'Hymn to Fire' by the Russian writer, Konstantin Balmont (1867-1942), which was translated into English in 1923.[2]

I think that probably what happened is that Edith came across the verse in the course of her studies in Literature and Drama. It is the sixth stanza of seven in the whole poem, and is indeed about a witch being burned to death.

---

[1]   op. cit. p. 123.

[2]   Babette Deutsch and Avrahm Yarminolinsky *Modern Russian Poetry - An Anthology* (John Lane - The Bodley Head, 1923) p. 79.

It differs from the verse as given in *Witchcraft Today* in that someone (almost certainly Gardner!) has left out words and lines in copying. The original verse is as follows:

> *I remember, O Fire,*
> *How thy flames once enkindled my flesh,*
> *Among writhing witches caught close in thy flame-woven mesh.*
> *How, tortured for having beheld what is secret,*
> *We were flung to the fire for the joy of our sabbath.*
> *But to those who had seen what we saw*
> *Yea, Fire was naught.*
> *Ah, well I remember*
> *The buildings ablaze where we burned*
> *In the fires we lit, and smiled to behold the flames wind*
> *About us, the faithful, among all the faithless and blind.*
> *To the chanting of prayers, the frenzy of flame,*
> *We sang thy hosannahs, oh strength-giving Fire:*
> *I pledged love to thee from the pyre!*

Having postulated quite definitely in the introduction to this book that there was no single moment when the witch cult was invented, I have begun to conceive of how the process of evolution may provide one explanation of what happened.

Essentially, it can be looked at as consisting of individuals getting to know each other, with individual friendships being formed, common interests shared and enthusiasms acquired. Gradually, a whole range of ideas began to be shared among the group, until a common philosophy and practice began to emerge, each individual having contributed towards the whole.

The individuals concerned were likely to have been Rosamund and George Sabine; Catherine Chalk; Dorothy Fordham; Katherine Oldmeadow; Edith Woodford-Grimes; Ernie, Susie and Rosetta Mason; and possibly other characters like Elsie Begg and Irene Lyon-Clark.

I must emphasise that, for most of the time that they knew each other, they were not a coven or at any rate did not call themselves such. They weren't all witches and they didn't all become witches. Some were on the fringe and some at the heart of what was going on. There was not, at least initially, a dividing line between those who considered themselves members of a coven and those who didn't, though this probably did happen later. The implications of an evolutionary approach is that asking the question "Was so-and-so a witch?" may not have been a relevant question.

That Rosamund thought of herself as a witch by the time she encountered Katherine Oldmeadow is shown by Katherine's change of attitude to witches which occurred at the same time.

Why Rosamund thought of herself as a witch I do not know, but I am going to attempt a possible explanation, although I freely admit that it is all pure speculation.

It started when she first met her future husband, George Sabine, probably in early 1905. As we have seen, she chose the 'sacramental name' of Vacuna after reading that Vacuna was a Sabine goddess.

I get the impression that Rosamund was someone who liked to explore new avenues of investigation, and I suspect that in looking into magical beliefs and practices in the area of central Italy she would have come across Charles Godfrey Leland's *Aradia, Gospel of the Witches*, first published in 1899.[3]

According to Professor Robert Mathiesen, in his introduction to the 2010 edition of *Aradia*, published by The Witches' Almanac, there was only one review of the book in English and that was in *Folk Lore* in 1900.[4] Rosamund could well have read that review or seen the book itself in one of her regular visits to Watkins bookshop.

---

[3]   Charles Godfrey Leland *Aradia, Gospel of the Witches* (David Nutt, 1899)
[4]   *Folk Lore* 11 (1900) p. 309.

In time, and exactly when I do not know, Rosamund began to think of herself as a witch and began to read avidly anything to do with the subject.

I suspect that this was intensified following the publication in 1921 of Margaret Murray's *The Witch Cult in Western Europe* and particularly following the review of that volume in the *Occult Review* the following year.[5]

The *Occult Review* was, according to the website of the International Association for the Preservation of Spiritualist and Occult Periodicals (IAPSOP):

> *... undoubtedly the pre-eminent English-language occult journal of the first quarter of the twentieth century because of the scope and quality of its contributors ...*[6]

And it was in the *Occult Review* that Rosamund's 1930 article 'Rose of the World' appeared.

Indeed, I suspect that it was with Brodie-Innes' article in the *Occult Review* that Rosamund came across the idea of the witch cult and began to see the possibilities of being a witch herself.

Brodie-Innes emphasised its universality when he wrote: "... the cult of the witch is as old as the world, and will last as long." And I think it was with witchcraft that Rosamund began to see an integrating principle that would put her various esoteric and practical interests into a fruitful context.

If so, it was, I am sure, focused on the idea that two people had both had memories of previous lives as witches, and/or had the idea that they might have had witch ancestry.

Who these were I do not know, but the evidence I gave in Chapter 17 demonstrates to my satisfaction that one person at least by

---

[5] J. W. Brodie Innes 'The Cult of the Witch' in *Occult Review* Vol 35 March 1922 pp. 150-163.

[6] http://www.iapsop.com

1925 considered themselves to be a witch and that individual was Rosamund Sabine.

As I said in the Introduction, witchcraft was just one of their interests. It was not their religion. They remained 'C of E', Catholic or of the Theosophical approach to life, although I think later, at least for Gerald and Edith, it did become increasingly like a religion.

So, we have a network of friends, some of whom know all the members of the group and some are perhaps friendly with only one. It could not at that stage be called a coven in any sense.

If we take seriously the idea that the witch cult developed as a result of the combination of the interests of the individuals concerned, then there is much that Katherine Oldmeadow in particular could have contributed. This would certainly have included an awareness of nature and nature spirits. She encouraged, and she was not alone in this, an awareness of the landscape of the Forest and of the trees and plants which grew there. She may have encouraged techniques for seeing the nature spirits, fairies and the subtle realms in general. Her keenness for dancing barefoot in the woods certainly harmonised with the desire to go skyclad by others in the group. And her enthusiasm for secret rituals in hidden places was certainly taken up by the emerging witch cult.

Professor Ronald Hutton has urged caution as to the extent to which the individuals I have identified were actually known to each other.[7] I agree that some of the links are not proven, but there is still, I am sure, more research which can be done which, in time, will prove or disprove the closeness or otherwise of those links.

They certainly each had particular interests which could have contributed to the whole. Rosamund had a background in ritual magic, herbalism and the use of psychic powers. The Mason family had an awareness and use of what might be called popular

---

[7] Ronald Hutton letter to the author 30th November 2019.

psychology, along with what have been called mind control techniques, plus the rituals and beliefs inherent in both Theosophy and Co-Masonry. Likewise, Edith could contribute her skills in elocution and performance as well as her considerable talents in writing and editing.

We can list at least some of their common interests in the esoteric field, such as magic, yoga, popular psychology, reincarnation, numerology and astrology, to name but a few.

I think, however, that there was a moment when those who either thought they had witch ancestry or had had a previous life as a witch, saw a spark igniting and the witch cult was born.

Let us imagine the scene. I suspect the thinking went somewhat as follows:

> *We believe we have witch blood, and we remember being witches in a previous lifetime. We were witches before. Therefore we can be witches again. In fact, we are witches and, moreover, some of us remember being witches together in past lifetimes. We are together in this lifetime. Therefore we can properly call ourselves a coven.*

This thinking on the part of the individuals concerned happened either over a period of several years from 1925 or may have taken place in a single moment of revelation to one individual who then inspired others to see something similar within themselves. This may have been as late as 1937.

It gradually grew upon them all that witchcraft was more than just another interest. It became the thread onto which the other interests of those involved were woven into something that we would recognise today.

It may well be that, as the idea of a coven became an enthusiasm, the practice of rituals began to hold their attention. Many would likely be spontaneous, but an initiation ritual would require more organising. Indeed, I think it may well have been the desire to bring Gerald Gardner into the group that provided the opportunity to create an initiation ritual. If so, he may well have been the very first ever to have been initiated into the wica.

So, in the next chapter we will look in more detail at that initiation and his relationship with his initiator, the witch he called Dafo.

But first, there is what we might call a snapshot of the group in early 1944, from Cecil Williamson, who ran the Museum of Magic and Witchcraft with Gerald Gardner on the Isle of Man ten years later.

He was part of 'Operation Fortitude' during the war. This was in the build-up to D-Day and was intended to deceive the German High Command by radio transmissions that the D-Day invasion would take place in the Pas-de-Calais rather than its actual location of Normandy.[8]

Williamson ended up on a site adjacent to The Naked Man, a prominent but dead tree in the heart of the New Forest.

48. The Naked Man in 2001

---

[8]   Roger Hesketh *Fortitude - The D-Day Deception Campaign* (St Ermin's Press, 1999).

Williamson had a:

... radio truck, 16 men and cooking and camping equipment ... 7 days a week and 24 hours a day, shunting non-existent troops and solving non-existent military cock up and vehicular crashes and breakdowns, actually all rather tedious and, after Day 3, dead boring.

But the weather was kind and so the good folk and the gentry toddled along to take a look, chat and to ask the normal questions. Being close to Brockenhurst we were never short of punters.

Then came the day when one retired ~~ex military type~~ civil servant and his good lady asked the 64$ question. Did we know why the site of our camp was called The Naked Man? Well, I did not, but was soon enlightened. Result - we both found that we had a common interest. Yes, you have guessed it: Witchcraft/Folklore.

Well, over the next several weeks I heard a lot about two New Forest covens and was introduced to a Mrs. Woodford Grimes. To be kind, one would call her middle-aged. Who was this lady? Well she was the ~~person with whom Gerald Gardner was dealing; of Gerald there was not a sighting.~~ Queen Bee of some social group, interested in the arts, music and folklore rituals. So it was that as the weeks passed Mrs Woodford Grimes would stop and chat on our common folklore interests of magic, making country charms and curses and of inherited know-how from long dead family ancestors. It all helped to pass the time. Then she would be up, off and away again. Yes, she kept her cards close to her chest. She lived in the area but never gave the address. She talked of her group in a general manner. Yes, there were men and women of her age group, all I gathered retired, but with a deep love and affection for Mother Nature. Yes, they did gather and do some simple forms of seasonal ritual celebration involving colour, movement and sounds, both intoned and musical. All rather sweet, neat and tidy - like her good tweed skirt, jacket and, of course, the pearls. Complete with sensible shoes to get one near or far as needs be in the

Forest. This in the midst of a war which at that time we looked like losing. You had to hand it to them. Slightly mad they may be to some. But to me they had spirit and deep emotional feeling for the wonder of the pulse of life found in all living things here on planet earth.[9]

Now, Cecil Williamson was known for exaggeration and telling deliberate untruths about Gerald Gardner and others. After all, his job during the war was precisely that. Nevertheless, there are things we can learn from this piece. First of all, the retired couple are probably George and Rosamund Sabine. They probably told Edith about Williamson and she decided to visit him.

According to Doreen Valiente the Naked Man had been somewhere the witches used to meet, and they may have been somewhat disconcerted to find that Williamson had set up his broadcasting unit at that very spot.

Williamson's description of Edith seems accurate enough, although he mentions her wearing pearls, which were generally associated with 'Old Dorothy', but it could well be that Edith had pearls as well.

After a gap of some 12 years or so, Williamson wrote a letter to Edith in late 1954 advising her about the financial aspects of running the museum on the Isle of Man and reminding her of their previous acquaintance. In her reply she does not deny this, but writes:

I am ... surprised that you remember me, as I am the sort of person who likes to go about affairs of interest in as unobtrusive a way as possible, so that many people who meet me do not really notice me, which is the way I prefer.[10]

However, Williamson's description of their beliefs and practices seems an honest and respectful view, one of the few we have.

9   Cecil Williamson - manuscript document in the possession of the author.
10 Letter from Edith Woodford-Grimes to Cecil Williamson 4 January 1955 in Boscastle Museum of Witchcraft.

22
The Most Wonderful Night of my Life

I wrote in Chapter 2 how Gerald Gardner referred to Edith Wood-ford-Grimes as "the witch" and, whilst there appeared to be others in the coven, she was the one who was closest to him and with whom he was in regular contact.

When I was carrying out research 20 years ago, I began to suspect that the relationship between Gerald and Dafo was more than just one of friendship and had become one of a more intimate nature.

I hinted at this in my book, *Wiccan Roots*[1] but it was Adrian Bott who first stated this unambiguously.[2]

I have written earlier that all the evidence points to Dafo as being the one who initiated Gerald Gardner.

And even before his initiation, Gerald had this to say about the small group of people with whom he had become friendly, and probably particularly Edith:

> *Now I was really very fond of them, and I knew that they had all sorts of magical beliefs. ... And I would have gone through hell and high water even then for any of them.*[3]

I have already mentioned Gerald's 1957 interview with Marjorie Proops, where she wrote:

> *I asked the doctor* [Gerald] *how he started. He said that twenty years ago he met a girl witch named Dafo and that was it. Dafo brought out the occult in Gerald.*[4]

[1] Philip Heselton (2000) pp. 262-267.
[2] Adrian Bott - The Great Wicca Hoax? in *White Dragon* Lughnasa 2001 pp. 13-15.
[3] Bracelin p. 165.
[4] Marjorie Proops I Got the Lowdown on this Witch Lark in *Daily Mirror* 10 April 1957.

Even though she was 51 years of age and only three years younger than Gerald he definitely saw her as a girl. Perhaps the use of the word 'girl' has changed since that time. Not only did she "bring out the occult" in Gerald, but I think that, as a result of the activities at the theatre, his initiation and the momentous rituals in the Forest to try to stop the threatened invasion, Gerald grew particularly close to Edith, as might be expected between those experiencing the depths of an initiation, particularly between the two directly involved. That this proximity turned to love is indicated by a comment made by Ralph Merrifield, of the Museum of London:

> ... in 1954, I received a visit at the Guildhall from [Gerald Gardner], and took the opportunity of asking where he had learned his witchcraft. His reply was "I fell in love with a witch when we were fire-watching together during the war."[5]

I think it clear from what I write below that the intimacy between Gerald and Edith occurred before the war had really started and while they may well have been fire-watching together, that would have been somewhat later.

Edith's grandson told me that she was directly involved in at least one of Gerald's books, as an editor, hacking it around. He told me that she had literary skills and could do this easily. Because of the timing, this is highly likely to have been *A Goddess Arrives*. I suspect that, after reading through the manuscript, she was quite blunt with Gerald, saying that it would need far more than just tinkering around with the grammar and spelling: it would need a complete re-write. However, she obviously thought it was worth doing.

I think a clue to Gerald's relationship with Edith is provided by a passage which appears in *A Goddess Arrives*:

---

5   Ralph Merrifield: G B Gardner and the 20th Century 'Witches' *Folklore Society News* no. 17 (June 1993) p. 10.

Dayonis and he [the hero of the story, Kinyras] *were constantly together and her quick observation and essentially practical mind saw deficiencies and made suggestions which were of real value to him. Their friendship and understanding of each other grew rapidly and he found her a charming, intelligent companion, one who would enter into his schemes and his moods in a way which he had never experienced with a woman before.*[6]

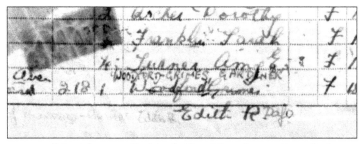

49. Extract from 1939 Register for Dennistoun Avenue, Somerford

The initial enumerator's record for Edith gives details that one would expect. No. 27 (now no. 16) Dennistoun Avenue, Somerford is given the house name of 'Theano', who was Pythagoras' wife, the part played by Edith at the Rosicrucian Theatre. Her name is given as Edith R. Woodford-Grimes; her date of birth 18th December 1887 and her occupation as Teacher of Elocution.

However, it seems as if there was plenty of opportunity for alteration of the original record and on most pages of the register there are examples of where an original entry has been amended.

Edith's entry is one which has been much amended. Her surname, "Woodford-Grimes", has been crossed out and, inserted above it is "WOODFORD-GRIMES, GARDNER". Also, the initial "R",

---

[6]   G. B. Gardner *A Goddess Arrives* (Arthur H. Stockwell, 1939) pp. 174-175.

which stands for Edith's middle name, Rose, has been crossed out and "Dafo" has been added.

One has to wonder what was going on. These were official alterations by the enumerator or other register official. Had Edith changed her surname? In no later document have I found the repeat of such a change. The fact that "Dafo" has been added suggests strongly that Gerald Gardner was the source of these changes. "Daff" was Edith's nickname within the family: "Dafo" seems to have been Gerald's own adaptation of that name.

So, what was going on? I would suggest that a strong possibility was that Gerald felt that he was in an intimate relationship with Edith, and that he therefore felt he had the right to propose alterations to the enumerator.

When had that intimacy occurred? I would suggest that it was something that happened earlier that same month, what Gerald has described as "the most wonderful night of my life": his initiation. He writes that if a couple carry out these rites together, fondness is apt to occur between the initiate and the initiator.[7]

Could this have happened between Gerald and Edith? Let us look at exactly what Gerald says:

> It was, I think, the most wonderful night of my life. In true witch fashion we had a dance afterwards, and kept it up until dawn.[8]

This always rather puzzled me. The picture of a group of witches dancing, presumably to music, for several hours until dawn in a house borrowed temporarily from its owner, struck me as being unlikely.

After seeing the 1939 Register entry, however, I began to suspect another explanation. And when I read that 'dance' was a colloquial

---

[7] Gardner (1954) p. 148.
[8] Bracelin p. 166.

expression for sexual intercourse, I felt reasonably sure that the explanation lay in that direction.

So now we can re-interpret that extract. "In true witch fashion": Gerald was obviously told by Edith that sexual intercourse was part of the initiation. I think she told him this to distance the act from being too personal, though obviously Gerald took it to be so and I suspect it was he who got the register entry altered. If I am right, this whole passage is typical of Gerald and a good example of 'double-entendre', where he writes something which can be interpreted one way but which is actually saying something quite different.

Indeed, less than 40 years ago, there was a tradition in north Yorkshire less than 10 miles from Edith's birthplace in Malton, that my friend, the late Amanda Class-Hamilton told me about. She was introduced to its members, who were old or middle-aged farming folk, but she was never initiated. One of the characteristics was that they practised sexual initiation. Edith's grandmother, Rosanna, lived even closer to the village where this tradition was centred, less than five miles, and I often wonder whether Edith could have been initiated into this tradition when young. We will probably never know.

The phrase "kept it up until dawn" clearly also has a sexual interpretation. To "keep it up" is a colloquial expression for a man keeping his erect penis in a woman's vagina for perhaps an extended period. This would doubtless have been familiar to Gerald from his working life out East, where such practices were traditional.

One can imagine the initiation ritual taking place with the others (probably members of the Mason family) present, who then withdrew, leaving Gerald and Edith alone. It is at this point that I suspect the sexual aspect of the ritual took place.

But what of Gerald's wife, Donna? He provides a clue himself when he says that when the war came:

> *Donna was called up as she was on the reserve of nurses. Nobody wanted me because of my age. I was an Air Raid Warden and that's all. I was more and more thrown upon my little group of friends.*[9]

The 1939 Register confirms this. Donna, under her full name of Dorothea F(rances) Gardner, was living at 86 Ebbisham Road, Epsom, Surrey, with Walter and Alice Scottow, presumably as a lodger. Her occupation is given as "Nurse, C.N.A., which stands for "Certified Nursing Assistant". She is also indicated as being in the Civil Nursing Reserve.

Donna had been living in London as a nurse before Gerald married her in 1927 and, whilst there were undoubtedly nursing opportunities in the Highcliffe area, perhaps the need for nurses was greatest in London and she had to go where she was sent, or perhaps she was not too unhappy to be away from Gerald for a while.

The Register also confirms that Gerald was living alone at Southridge, apart from two lodgers, William and Amelia Fribbens.

We know that later in the war Donna returned to Southridge, for we have an account by Maidie Doohan, who was a schoolgirl at the time and whose mother knew the Gardners. She told Ian Stevenson, the local historian:

> *I knew his [Gerald's] wife. She reminded me of a little sparrow. She was very, very short, almost black hair, very tiny, very petite person ... I never ever saw them even go out together. She seemed to live quite a different life. ... She was a very shy person. Well, she struck me as being shy. [She] never seemed to have any friends ... and I think it used to concern my mother, because she used to think that*

---

9   Bracelin p. 164.

perhaps she'd be a little lonely, you know, because she didn't seem to have any friends.[10]

Donna is always spoken of as being a really nice person, but someone who didn't particularly want to get involved in Gerald's witchcraft activities. Indeed, there is a hint of this in *Witchcraft Today*. After writing about married or other couples, Gerald says:

There are ... some unattached people, or some whose respective spouses are for some reason or another not members of the cult. I have heard fierce purists declare that no married man or woman should belong to, or attend, any club or society to which their respective partners did not also belong; but such strict views are not part of witchcraft.[11]

Donna, who seems to have been liked by everybody, was, I am sure, aware of Gerald's relationship with Edith. Whilst one might have expected that, being the daughter, grand-daughter, niece and sister of clergymen, she would have had a conventional attitude to Gerald's relationship with Edith, this does not seem to have been the case.

Indeed, Cecil Williamson (admittedly not the most reliable of sources) wrote to the late Mike Howard, Editor of *The Cauldron*:

... as she [Donna] *told my wife and myself she could not care less how many naked women Gerald played around with or what he got up to so long as she was not called upon to take part.*[12]

Aidan Kelly puts Donna's attitude into context:

One may wonder what [Gerald's] *wife, Donna, thought of all this. The pattern for the middle-class English wife was to keep her mouth shut and find a way to live with the problem; she might regret that she was not her husband's*

---

[10] Interview Maidie Doohan and Ian Stevenson 8 April 2005.

[11] Gardner (1954) p. 29.

[12] Letter Cecil Williamson to Mike Howard 25 February 1997 in Boscastle Museum of Witchcraft archives.

fantasized ideal woman, yet also recognize that, as a merely real and imperfect woman, there was no way that she could live up to that fantasy. Some wives would whip their husbands' bare butts in order to have sex. Others would give their husbands permission to meet their needs however they could, and would settle for enjoying the side-effects. Others, to be sure, would give up sex entirely. I am, of course, speculating here, and generalizing from very little data - for there has never been, as far as I know, an objective attempt at a scientific study of this question. But given all this, we can reasonably suppose that after a dozen years of trying to cope with Gerald's sexual problems, Donna might have been glad, or at least relieved, to have him find another path that could meet his needs. All the evidence about her is that, although not involved in the Craft herself, she never interfered with his Craft activity during their last twenty years together.[13]

That Gerald and Edith's relationship continued into 1940 is evidenced by two events which occurred in August of that year.

Firstly, Gerald was the one who gave Edith's daughter, Rosanne, away at her wedding. It is clear from this that Edith's marriage must have broken down completely, since it would normally be her husband's role to do this. Gerald is described as 'a close friend'.[14] Rosanne, aged 19, married Cecil Albert Thompson, known as Tommy, on Saturday 17th August 1940 at Christchurch Priory. The reception, which was attended by between 50 and 60 guests, was held at the Nelson Hotel, Mudeford which, perhaps significantly, was only 100 yards from the New Forest naturist club at Rushford Warren.

To coincide with Rosanne's wedding, Edith had taken the opportunity to move into a new house, Avenue Cottage, in Avenue

---

13 Aidan A. Kelly *Inventing Witchcraft* (Thoth Publications, 2007) p. 60.
14 *Christchurch Times* 24 August 1940.

Road, Highcliffe, leaving Rosanne and Tommy to live in Theano. The address of Avenue Cottage is sometimes given as Walkford, as it is between there and Highcliffe. It was only just over half a mile's walk from Southridge and, of course, Rosamund and George Sabine lived just down the same road at Whinchat. Avenue Cottage was rather larger than its name might suggest and was, in fact, a substantial house with a long garden, the bottom part of which extended behind neighbouring gardens on both sides. Edith also owned one of the neighbouring houses, letting it to tenants.

How could a modest teacher of elocution afford such a property? Edith's mother, Caroline, had died in March 1939, but the likelihood of any financially significant legacy from that direction is very low. Firstly, Edith's father had been an agricultural engineer and his income could not have been great. Secondly, any financial legacy would very likely be shared amongst the surviving six children. Edith's grandson believes that Gerald financed the whole enterprise, a conclusion which I had already reached independently. If so, it is another indication of how close Gerald and Edith were at that time.

The most commonly held view as to how Gerald and Edith met, as I mentioned in Chapter 2, is that given in *Gerald Gardner Witch*, which is that it was at the Rosicrucian Theatre run by the Crotona Fellowship in Christchurch. However, there has been a persistent rumour that they knew each other at an earlier date. Doreen Valiente wrote:

> *I have the impression ... that the connection between Brickett* [sic] *Wood and the Craft goes back for some time before I met Gerald, because he and Dafo used to go there.*[15]

---

[15] Letter Doreen Valiente to Mike Howard 24 March 1997 in Boscastle Museum of Witchcraft archives.

It is an intriguing possibility that Gerald may have met Edith at a naturist club in the London area.

Gerald retired to London in April 1936. Edith had probably left her husband some time that same year and may well have decided to get away from the Southampton area altogether and that London might provide the opportunities for her to use her skills to earn a living. Rosanne was aged 15, old enough, I suspect Edith felt, to be left living with Samuel.

This is, of course, all pure speculation and the only evidence that I have is an anonymous contribution to the *Sun Bathing Review*,[16] a naturist magazine. I set out below extracts from that article and also from letters by Edith. I am not by any means an expert in linguistic analysis, but this does seem to have a similarity with Edith's distinctive way of writing. Let us look first at extracts from some of Edith's letters:

> *I am not insensible to the many privileges I have received from Co-Freemasonry.*[17]

> *Thank you for your letter and good wishes for 1955; it was one of the many surprises one receives at times when the exchange of greetings is in the air.*[18]

> *Although I lead a simple, homely but very busy life that does not prevent my thinking about many things which have no bearing on my everyday life, the activities you write of come under the latter heading. ... furthermore, dissention is maintained at such a pitch throughout certain circles that I have no wish to be party to it.*[19]

Compare this with an extract from the anonymous piece in *Sun Bathing Review*:

[16] The Fouracres Club: A Feminine Member's Impression *Sun Bathing Review* August/September 1936.
[17] Edith Woodford-Grimes Draft letter to the Grand Secretary, International Co-Freemasonry July 1935 - in Toronto Collection.
[18] Edith Woodford-Grimes Letter to Cecil Williamson 4 January 1955 in Boscastle Museum of Witchcraft archives.
[19] Edith Woodford-Grimes Letter to Charles Cardell 26 July 1959.

SPRING! Bluebells - green leaves. Eighteen miles in a car can show the Londoner no more striking contrast in "atmosphere" than that between the stiffness, stuffiness, artificiality and conventions of town life and the freedom, ease and naturalness of Fouracres.

*In the town - hard paved, evil smelling streets, permeated with the fumes of petrol; soot-smeared houses, begrimed as soon as painted; and a few tired trees struggling into their spring clothes, only to be sooted as soon as donned.
...*

Sitting round the lawn in groups, many are the interesting discussions that can arise from quite a casual remark, and sometimes startling is the contrast of opinions revealed, which open up new fields for the thoughtful.[20]

It seems to me that there is a certain similarity of "feel" between this and the extracts from Edith's letters. It could be characterised as a certain distance between the writer and her subject matter.

Former Oxford academic, Francis Cameron, who has taken an interest in Dafo and whom I consulted over this matter, brings up another point:

... it was the semi-colons in the Fouracres piece that struck me on my first reading. ... it's not possible to be completely certain but I do feel [Edith] and the writer of the Fouracres piece share a similar enjoyment in the use of the semi-colon.[21]

When I think back over the whole of my reading career, right back to my earliest memories from my schooldays - and I have always been a voracious reader - I have to say the use of semicolons is rather rare. The text where they appear most often is the Authorised Version of the Bible - and that's probably where my own usage has its origin.

---

[20]   The Fouracres Club: A Feminine Member's Impression *Sun Bathing Review* August/September 1936.
[21]   Email Francis Cameron to the author 23 November 2010.

I do not remember semicolons being introduced as any part of a school lesson. Nor am I aware of reading about how they should (or should not) be used.

So when I come across semicolons in print I tend to take particular notice of them. For me, they tend to stick out, to call for my attention - because they are a rarity. When I read the Feminine Member's Impression I noticed the neat way in which her use of semicolons separated the elements of the list of attributes.[22]

Now, I think it likely that Dafo was a naturist and a member of the New Forest Club. Unfortunately, membership records of that club have been lost, but we have already noted that she used to practise yoga in the nude. Also, her daughter, Rosanne, had her wedding reception in the Nelson Inn, a mere 100 yards from the New Forest Club, and several of her wedding presents were from prominent members of the New Forest Club.

On the basis of this information, I think a reasonable case could be made for both Edith and Rosanne being members of the New Forest Club. However, whether they had been members before meeting Gerald Gardner remains completely unresolved.

Now, the New Forest Club was not in the New Forest but near it. I have previously quoted Bracelin as writing that "the only place in England where he had friends was the region of the New Forest".[23] If, as I had earlier speculated, these were David and Com, he would be likely to have simply said "Bournemouth". If he had friends who were members of the New Forest Club, including, notably, Edith, then the phrase "the region of the New Forest" would be just the thing to use about members of the New Forest Club, without revealing anything about his naturist connections.

However, ultimately, the question for the moment remains open.

---

[22] Email Francis Cameron to the author 27 November 2010.
[23] Bracelin p. 159.

End Word

One of my aims in carrying out the research for this book was to see whether any of the individuals that we have identified as being in the group into which Gerald Gardner was initiated (the so-called New Forest Coven) might have brought some elements through from what has been called 'traditional witchcraft', which in our case can be defined as something which existed independently of Gerald Gardner or the group into which he was initiated.

There is a whole body of literature relating to traditional witchcraft, which postulates that there is a traditional type of witchcraft. Books such as Michael Howard's *Children of Cain*[1]; David Clarke and Andy Roberts' *Twilight of the Celtic Gods*[2]; and Paul Pearson and Tallis Harrill's *The Mountain and the Stream*[3] give varying degrees of detail about some of these traditions, which are usually extremely secretive and a degree of trust is necessary before anything is revealed to researchers such as myself.

I do not, in the present volume, put forward anything but the most tentative ideas as to whether the individuals who feature in this book have backgrounds in any such traditional craft.

We can now take a fresh look at the question posed earlier - Did the witch cult have roots back in time in traditional witchcraft or was it invented by the members we have already identified in more recent times?

The short answer is 'yes' and 'yes'!

---

[1] Michael Howard *Children of Cain - A Study of Modern Traditional Witches* (Three Hands Press, 2011).
[2] David Clarke with Andy Roberts *Twilight of the Celtic Gods - An Exploration of Britain's Hidden Pagan Traditions* (Blandford, 1996).
[3] Paul Pearson and Tallis Harrill *The Mountain and the Stream - Rural Animism and Pagan Practices* (Windgather Publishing, 2017).

Mary Kay Mahoney has done a lot of research using online resources into the ancestry of some of the people I have been
looking at in this book.⁴ Her researches have saved me a lot of
time and, for example, the Wilde connection referred to in Chapter 11 was her discovery.

She believes that there were several witch families down the ages
and that there were numerous connections, of which this is but
one example.

I am open to the possibility that some of the individuals I am looking at may have had witch ancestry. Gerald Gardner and others in
the group believed they had such ancestry. To be honest, the evidence is still very uncertain. However, I do include an account of
what appears to be a traditional group very close to Dafo's birthplace. And I do feel that there is evidence for traditional witchcraft
in Sussex, building on the work of Doreen Valiente and Ralph
Harvey and my own ongoing researches.

Also, whilst it seems likely that the rituals to stop the invasions
of the Spanish Armada and Napoleon, to name but two, may have
taken place, the individuals, families and groups involved may not
necessarily have referred to themselves as witches.

However, we can approach things from a different perspective,
which I am now convinced is a more realistic view of how things
were.

It is a matter of what we might call 'continuous evolution' where
all of the participants contributed something towards the whole,
according to their particular knowledge, background, skills and
insights.

So, to answer the question: who invented 'Wicca' - Doreen Valiente, Gerald Gardner, Dafo, Dorothy, Katherine Oldmeadow,
Rosamund? The only honest answer is "all of them"!

---

⁴ Mary Kay Mahoney personal communications with the author.

I sometimes feel that it was like a car that refuses to start. Gerald was so enthusiastic about not letting the witch cult die out that, following his initiation, he started to plan what became *High Magic's Aid* just ten years later. And two years after that he co-operated with Cecil Williamson in opening a Museum of Magic and Witchcraft on the Isle of Man.

But his attempts to initiate new blood into the witch cult had been disappointing. His first initiate, Barbara Vickers, had lost interest, and the only other initiate that we know about by 1954, Doreen Valiente, found it difficult to travel frequently from her home in Bournemouth.

Gerald had re-erected the half-timbered building known as the Witches' Cottage on land he owned next to the Fiveacres naturist club and had persuaded some of the members of the club to join him in rituals, but I suspect that they were never that enthusiastic and by the time *Witchcraft Today* was published in 1954, there was probably very little going on, either there or in Highcliffe.

In the exhibit captions in his museum, Gerald refers to what appear to be two covens as "The Southern Coven of British Witches" and "The Northern Coven". In both cases, the use of the word 'coven' is rather exaggerated. The former was the remnants of the original group into which he was initiated, of which I suspect Edith to have been the only active surviving member.

I was puzzled for a long time as to the identity of the "Northern Coven". Was it perhaps some surviving group in the Liverpool area? I gradually came to realise that it was none other than the coven he was trying, rather unsuccessfully, to form at Bricket Wood. I had fallen into the trap deliberately set by Gerald. It was not by any means in the North of England, but simply north of Highcliffe!

Gerald felt that at least he had tried, but I think he saw *Witchcraft Today* as something of a farewell message. There is a poignant passage towards the end of the book:

> *... I think we must say good-bye to the witch. The cult is doomed, I am afraid, partly because of modern conditions, housing shortage, the smallness of modern families, and chiefly by education. The modern child is not interested. He knows witches are all bunk - and there is the great fear. I have heard it said: 'I'd simply love to bring Diana in, she would adore it and she has the powers, I know; but suppose in some unguarded moment she let it out at school that I was a witch? They would bully and badger her, and the County Council or somebody would come round and take her away from me and send her to an approved school. They do such awful things by these new laws nowadays. ..."*
> *Diana will grow up and have love affairs, is not interested, or is interested but gets married and her husband is not interested, and so the coven dies out or consists of old and dying people.*
>
> *The other reason is that science has displaced her; good weather reports, good health services, outdoor games, bathing, nudism, the cinema and television have largely replaced what the witch had to give. Free thought or spiritualism, according to your inclinations, have taken away the fear of Hell that she prevented, though nothing yet has replaced her greatest gifts: peace, joy and content.*[5]

It is, perhaps, ironic that this swan song by Gardner, which resulted in due course in adverse publicity in the more sensational Sunday papers, was to lead, contrary to what those newspapers intended, to an influx of people interested in finding out more about, and ultimately joining, the witch cult. These enabled it not only to survive but to grow into the worldwide religion which it is today.

---

[5] Gardner (1954) p. 129.

Bibliography

Begg, R. Burns *Trials for Witchcraft in Scotland in 1661 and 1662*

Belloc, Hilaire *The Four Men: A Farrago* (Thomas Nelson and Sons, 1911)

Benney, Clive *The Secrets of Rosemundy House* (Wheal Hawke Publications 2014)

Bourne, Lois *Dancing with Witches* (Robert Hale, 1998)

Bracelin, J.L. *Gerald Gardner Witch* (Octagon, 1960)

Brandwood, Geoff (ed.) *Living, Leisure and Law: Eight Building Types in England 1800-1941* (Spire Books, in association with the Victorian Society, 2010)

Clarke, David with Roberts, Andy *Twilight of the Celtic Gods - An Exploration of Britain's Hidden Pagan Traditions* (Blandford, 1996)

Crawford, Elizabeth *Enterprising Women: The Garretts and their Circle* (Francis Boutle Publishers, 2002)

Brodie-Innes, J.W. *Scottish Witchcraft Trials* (The Chiswick Press, 1891)

Credland, Arthur G. *Shipping Posters and Graphic Works: Harry Hudson Rodmell 1896-1984* (Hull City Museums and Hutton Press, 1999)

Crowther, Arnold *Witchcraft and the Scots* (The Doreen Valiente Foundation in association with the Centre for Pagan Studies, 2018)

Crowther, Patricia *One Witch's World* (Hale, 1998)

Deutsch, Babette and Yarminolinsky, Avrahm *Modern Russian Poetry* (John Lane - The Bodley Head, 1923)

Farrar, Janet and Stewart *Eight Sabbats for Witches* (Hale, 1981)

Farrar, Janet and Stewart *The Witches' Way* (Hale, 1984)

Gardner, G.B. *Keris and Other Malay Weapons* (Progressive Publishing Company, Singapore, 1936)

Gardner, G.B. *A Goddess Arrives* (Arthur H Stockwell, 1939)

Gardner, G.B. (writing as Scire) *High Magic's Aid* (Michael Houghton, 1949)

Gardner, Gerald B. *Witchcraft Today* (Rider, 1954)

Gardner, G.B. *The Story of the Famous Witches Mill at Castletown, Isle of Man* (The Photochrom Co. Ltd., 1958)

Gardner, G.B. *The Meaning of Witchcraft* (Aquarian, 1959)

Gilbert, R.A. *The Golden Dawn Companion* (Aquarian, 1986)

Gosse, Aimée Bothwell *The Rose Immortal* (Rider, 1916)

Grimassi, Raven *The Witches' Craft - The Roots of Witchcraft and Magical Transformation* (Llewellyn, 2005)

Haywood, Colonel A. and Clarke, Brigadier F.A.S. *The History of the Royal West African Force* (Gale and Polden, 1964)

Henslow, T. Geoffrey W. *The Rose Encyclopaedia* (Vickery, Kyle and Co. Ltd., 1922)

Herringshaw, Sheila D. *A Portrait of Highcliffe* (Sheila D Herringshaw, 1981)

Heselton, Philip *Wiccan Roots* (Capall Bann, 2000)

Heselton, Philip *Gerald Gardner and the Cauldron of Inspiration* (Capall Bann 2003)

Heselton, Philip *Witchfather: A Life of Gerald Gardner* 2 vols. (Thoth Publications, 2012)

Heselton, Philip *Doreen Valiente Witch* (The Doreen Valiente Foundation in association with the Centre for Pagan Studies, 2016)

Hesketh, Roger *Fortitude - The D-Day Deception Campaign* (St. Ermin's Press, 1999)

Howard, Michael *Children of Cain - A Study of Modern Traditional Witches* (Three Hands Press, 2011)

Hutton, Ronald *The Triumph of the Moon* (Oxford University Press, 1999; Revised edition 2019)

James, A.G.F. Eliot *Our Servants, their duties to us and ours to them* (Ward Lock, 1883)

Johns, June *King of the Witches* (Peter Davies, 1969)

Juers, Evelyn *The Recluse* (Giramondo Publishing, 2012)

Kelly, Aidan A. *Inventing Witchcraft* (Thoth Publications, 2007)

Kitcher, Reg *My Early Years at Hinton Admiral and Highcliffe, Hampshire 1910-1939* (Olive J. Samuel, 1985)

Lee-Van den Daele, Richard and Beale, R. David *Milner Field: The Lost Country House of Titus Salt Jnr* (Barleybrook, 2013)

Leland, Charles Godfrey *Aradia, Gospel of the Witches* (David Nutt, 1899)

McIntosh, Christopher *The Rosicrucians - The History, Mythology and Rituals of an Esoteric Order* (Aquarian, 1980; revised edition Weiser, 1997)

Mathers, S. Liddell MacGregor *The Key of Solomon the King* (George Redway, 1888)

Milne, A.A. *Winnie-the-Pooh* (Methuen, 1926)

Munro, Rona *The Last Witch* (Nick Hern Books, 2009)

Murray, Margaret Alice *The Witch-Cult in Western Europe: A Study in Anthropology* (Oxford, 1921)

Oldmeadow, Ernest *The North Sea Bubble* (Grant Richards, 1906)

Oldmeadow, Katherine *Madcap Judy* (Collins, 1919)

Oldmeadow, Katherine *Princess Candida* (Collins, 1922)

Oldmeadow, Katherine *Princess Charming* (Collins, 1923)

Oldmeadow, Katherine *Princess Anne* (Collins, 1925)

Oldmeadow, Katherine (writing as Pamela Grant) *The Fortunes of Billy* (Collins, 1925)

Oldmeadow, Katherine *Princess Elizabeth* (Collins, 1926)

Oldmeadow, Katherine *When George III was King* (Hutchinson, 1934)

Oldmeadow, Katherine *The Folklore of Herbs* (Cornish Bros., 1946)

Oldmeadow, Katherine *The Fortunes of Jacky* (The Children's Press, 1957)

Pearson, Paul and Harrill, Tallis *The Mountain and the Stream - Rural Animism and Pagan Practices* (Windgather Publishing, 2017)

Pécastaing-Boissière, Muriel *Annie Besant (1847-1933) Struggles and Quest* (Theosophical Publishing House, 2017)

Ramacharaka, Yogi *Advanced Course in Yogi Philosophy and Oriental Occultism* (Fowler, 1905)

Rippon, Nicola *The Plot to Kill Lloyd George - The Story of Alice Wheeldon and the Pear Tree Conspiracy* (Wharncliffe Books, 2009)

Samuel, Olive J. *Chewton Bunny, Highcliffe - The History of a Romantic Glen* (Olive J. Samuel, 1986)

Scire (G B Gardner) *High Magic's Aid* (Michael Houghton, 1949)

Sharpe, Charles Kirkpatrick *A Historical Account of the Belief of Witchcraft in Scotland* (Hamilton Adams & Co., Thomas D. Morrison, 1884)

Sheldrick, Albert A. *A Different World: Ashwell before 1939* (Cortney, n.d.)

Tapsell, Jonathan *Ameth: The Life and Times of Doreen Valiente* (Avalonia, 2014)

Tapsell, Jonathan *Psychic Jungle* (Lilith Mandrake Books, 2015)

Tarn, John Nelson *Five Per Cent Philanthropy* (Cambridge University Press, 1973)

Taylor, Anne *Annie Besant: A Biography* (Oxford University Press, 1992)

Thompson, Edward (ed.) *The Poems and Miscellaneous Compositions of Paul Whitehead With Explanatory Notes Of His Writings* (S. Price, W. Watson, et al, 1777)

Tite, Graham *Six Pence and a Rose: Summers Place and Sussex History* (Sotheby's, 1986)

Valiente, Doreen *The Rebirth of Witchcraft* (Robert Hale, 1989)

Walton, Veronica (Ed.) *Beatrice of Bolderwood - The Diary of a New Forest Girl 1899* (New Forest Ninth Centenary Trust, 2004)

Wodehouse, P.G. *The Inimitable Jeeves* (Herbert Jenkins, 1923)

Index

CPSIA information can be obtained
at www.ICGtesting.com
Printed in the USA
LVHW080410180820
663426LV00020B/988